MANAGING PILOT STRESS

MANAGING PILOT STRESS

Michael Thomas, Ph.D.

AN ELEANOR FRIEDE BOOK

Macmillan Publishing Company / New York
Collier Macmillan Publishers / London

Macmillan Publishing Company
866 Third Avenue, New York, NY 10022
Collier Macmillan Canada, Inc.

Library of Congress Cataloging-in-Publication Data
Thomas, Michael, 1957–
Managing Pilot Stress/ by Michael Thomas.
p. cm.
"An Eleanor Friede book."
Bibliography: p.
Includes index
ISBN 0-02-617760-9
1. Air pilots—Health and hygiene. 2. Stress (Psychology)
3. Stress (Physiology) I. Title.
RC1063.T46 1989
616.9'80213-dc19   89-2506   CIP

Macmillan books are available at special discounts for bulk
purchases for sales promotions, premiums, fund-raising, or
educational use. For details, contact:

Special Sales Director
Macmillan Publishing Company
866 Third Avenue
New York, NY 10022

10 9 8 7 6 5 4 3 2 1

Design by Claudia Carlson

Printed in the United States of America

*This book is dedicated to those pilots
whose collective thoughts and actions
have brought into existence
the third revolution
in aviation safety.*

CONTENTS

ACKNOWLEDGMENTS

There are a number of people whom I would like to thank for their part in the development of this book. First, I would like to thank my mother, Evelyn, for her support and for providing an ear and words of encouragement. I would like to thank my father, John, who said "OK" when I told him that I wanted to learn to fly. I would also like to extend thanks to my brother, John, Jr., who has always been in my corner.

And there are those special people who made my career in aviation possible. To W. T. Washington, my Civil Air Patrol instructor, who spent many patient hours with me on the ground and in the air, and to Mary Gormley, my Civil Air Patrol squadron commander, I can only say "thank you" and know that who I am today has been greatly influenced by the two of you.

My knowledge and skills in aviation, psychology, and human resources development are the tools that I must work with. To my flight instructors and college professors, I am greatly indebted.

I would also like to thank my close friends and flying companions, Steve Gideon, John Inzerella, and Richard

Stone, whose friendship and support have meant a lot to me. Other friends and colleagues who receive my expression of gratitude are Melinda Seger-Gideon, David and Diane Salzman, Louise Wesner, Richard Miller, Donald Cordier, Marla Hollander, Luiza Jatoba, and my friends and colleagues at Somos Amigos.

Carolyn Satzman, thank you for your professional support and guidance. You were instrumental in helping me to conceptualize pilot stress in the framework of a syndrome.

I would like to also thank Anita Rosenfield, my typist, for making miracles happen.

To my publisher, Eleanor Friede, who coined the term "Pilot/Author Stress Syndrome," thank you for your acknowledgment and for the long tedious hours of your time spent reading and editing my manuscript. And to Barbara Bowen, I would also like to thank you. Your support was very helpful.

Others who provided professional assistance that I am grateful to are Barbara Snyder, whose knowledge of medicine greatly contributed to parts of this book; and Tracy Benedict, who also provided editorial assistance.

Finally, I would like to extend thanks to all of my aviation clients, students, and colleagues. And to those pilots who candidly expressed their thoughts and feelings, I would like to give my acknowledgment and thanks, for without your input, this book would not have been possible.

INTRODUCTION

It is generally agreed in the aviation community that approximately 80% of all aviation accidents and 60% of all fatal aviation accidents are caused by human error. But what does the term "human error" actually mean? It appears to be less harsh than the common label, "pilot error," with which we are all familiar. However, close examination of these terms exposes them as catchall phrases that are descriptive only of what has already occurred. They fail to explain the reasons why pilots err in the first place. They also inspire criticism of the pilot, who is often an innocent victim of circumstances which lead to errors in the cockpit.

A number of years ago I became interested in understanding the causality of the often fatal errors made in aircraft cockpits. I was intrigued by the fact that many of these errors are made by highly trained, skilled, and experienced professional pilots, flying state-of-the-art equipment. It wasn't until I experienced a bout of aviation-related stress that I had even considered looking into this matter further.

I had been turned on to aviation since childhood. All

I ever wanted to do in life was to become a professional pilot. At the age of twenty-three I was a successful charter pilot, and yet I was burnt out. My stress was so great that I was ready to give up my dreams and retire from aviation. There were no simple answers to explain my feelings of incompetence, anger, depression, victimization, guilt, and fatigue, so I embarked on a personal exploration to understand these stress reactions.

Other pilots shared my thoughts and feelings. They confided in me and spoke of their personal experiences with stress. Some of the pilots were only beginning to see the signs of stress in their personal and professional lives, while others were affected more seriously. Realizing that other pilots could identify with my stress experience, I conducted an investigation that lasted seven years. This investigation led me to discover stress-related response patterns among pilots that had previously not been acknowledged in the professional literature. I realized that this information could dramatically affect the field of aviation safety.

I have come to recognize my personal-life crisis as an important opportunity. It allowed me to discover the Stress Syndrome, which explains many of the underlying causes of human error in the cockpit.

As an aviation safety consultant, I have led numerous seminars on the subject and have had the opportunity to talk with hundreds of pilots about their experiences. As a psychotherapist, I specialize in the problems that pilots and their families face. I have had the opportunity to help pilots confront the issues in their lives which lead to Pilot Stress Syndrome, and to contribute to their effective management of the syndrome.

My research suggests that the effects of Pilot Stress Syndrome are widespread. I strongly believe that all pilots either have been, currently are, or will be affected to some degree by this potentially dangerous syndrome. No pilot is immune to its effects.

I do not, however, claim that Pilot Stress Syndrome explains all causation in pilot-induced aviation accidents and incidents. Such a claim would be grandiose, false, and misleading, and would only limit further inquiry in the field of aviation safety. My observations are presented as an addition to the existing body of aviation safety knowledge available to the professional pilot. *Managing Pilot Stress* examines the causes and effects of this syndrome, and provides a practical approach for its management, including the techniques successfully used with airline, corporate, military, and general aviation pilots.

For the sake of clarity, this book uses the generic term "pilot" or "pilots" to represent all flight crewmembers (captain, first officer, flight engineer, etc.), and those pilots who engage in flight for purposes other than air commerce (general aviation, military, etc.). To reduce redundancy, the pilot is referred to in the masculine form, except in those cases where female pilots are specifically addressed. In 1986 43,082 of the 709,118 active certificated pilots were women. Of these pilots, 1,334 women held Airline Transport Pilot Ratings. With the rapid expansion of professional aviation, the number of active certificated women pilots continues to grow. As we can see by these figures, female pilots are an important part of aviation and will be acknowledged as such in this book. Pilot Stress Syndrome affects all pilots, and though the examples provided in this book will lean toward commercial aviation, these concepts are equally applicable to all sectors of aviation, and all levels of pilot experience.

The material presented in this book has been compiled from various sources including my own observations and experiences as a professional pilot. As a psychotherapist and an aviation safety consultant, I have interviewed hundreds of pilots from virtually every sector of aviation. I have worked with families of pilots and extensively reviewed professional literature from the fields of aviation, psychology, and medicine.

All case histories and interviews presented here are authentic. They represent the true thoughts and feelings of pilots, although their statements are presented in a manner that maintains anonymity for both the pilot and his company. The goal of this book is to help pilots benefit from the experiences of other pilots, and through an understanding of the pilot stress discoveries, enjoy a safe and fulfilling future in aviation.

—MICHAEL THOMAS, PH.D.

I

PILOT STRESS:
THE SYNDROME

1

Pilot Stress

The airliner is cruising at 37,000 feet. The sky is clear and it is a beautiful day over the Arizona desert. Outside the cockpit window, the crew of the Boeing 727 can see the expanse of red clay that comprises the jagged terrain, nearly seven miles below.

Everything has been going as scheduled, and it appears that the flight will be a routine one, until the first officer suddenly makes a startling announcement in a controlled but urgent tone.

"I smell smoke."

As he speaks he notices that he is rapidly becoming tense, his heart is pounding, and he has begun to sweat.

The captain and flight engineer, both realizing that where there's smoke there's fire, also become tense.

"Where's the smoke?" asks the captain, his heart also pounding.

"I don't know. I just smell smoke." The first officer is sniffing rapidly to determine the source of the smoke.

The flight engineer speaks up.

"I'm not sure if I smell it or not. What does it smell like? Electrical, air conditioning, what?" He searches his panel to see if anything looks abnormal.

"I think it's electrical," the first officer replies. By now the captain and first officer are frantically sniffing around their panels. The flight engineer begins checking for popped circuit breakers in a frantic attempt to determine the source of the smoke. Within moments he too, smells the smoke.

"I think it's electrical. Can't see anything up here. How about you guys?"

The other two crewmembers are unable to detect the source.

The flight engineer begins to progressively isolate each part of the electrical system to determine the exact location of the smoke. He carefully follows the emergency checklist, as the captain and the first officer continue to search their stations for any sign of smoke.

The captain tells the crew, "Let me know what's going on," as he continues monitoring the routine aspects of the flight.

The flight engineer diligently follows the procedures as prescribed in the emergency checklist. As he progressively isolates each of the aircraft's systems, the other crewmembers wait in strained anticipation. They are counting on him to solve the potentially dangerous problem that they are faced with. The flight engineer pulls a circuit breaker and pauses.

"Has the smoke stopped?" He still smells it.

The first officer speaks up. "It seems to be getting stronger." There's a tone of urgency in his voice. The others feel the pressure coming on.

"I think you're right," the flight engineer reluctantly confirms.

"Let's see—closing the generator switches." He slowly resets each of the components of the aircraft's systems. Then he continues to isolate others. Finally, when he pulls the standby battery circuit breaker the smoke stops. "I think it's stopped," the captain announces. His words are filled with caution and hope.

The flight engineer begins resetting the standby battery circuit breaker.

"We'd better be sure."

As he completes this task the smoke returns.

"Bingo, there's the culprit."

They all feel a deep sense of relief as he pulls the faulty circuit breaker, cutting off the source of the smoke. He then restores the functioning components of the electrical system. As he does this, each crewmember feels the stress decreasing. They begin to feel less tense and more relaxed.

The above scenario is one which every airline pilot has experienced in the flight simulator, and some have experienced in actual flight conditions. Despite the type of aircraft flown, smoke in the cockpit is a standard emergency procedure which every flight crewmember must learn to handle effectively.

As you read the scenario, you probably found yourself experiencing some of the same physiological and emotional responses as the cockpit crewmembers—such as increased heart rate, anxiety, and muscular tension. You may have also noticed emotional reactions of urgency, fear, hope, and relief. You are not alone if you experienced any of these reactions. Most pilots report experiencing subjectively noticeable physiological and emotional changes during simulated and actual emergencies.

The scenario addresses an emergency situation. Most of us recognize that stress is a natural consequence of such an experience for the pilot; but many pilots aren't aware that stress is with us even when the pressure is not on. The pilot is affected by stress even when there is no immediate threat of danger.

HOW PILOTS VIEW STRESS

When most pilots think of the term "stress," their thoughts become focused on the obvious physiological changes that accompany stress. To a much lesser degree, there is consideration of the psychological effects that can be present. Usually long-term damaging effects aren't even considered. A thirty-one-year-old first officer I interviewed demonstrated this:

> Yes, I know what stress is. I feel it when the pressure's on. I don't know how I can describe it for sure—but I just know it's there. I feel run down, nervous and sometimes a little confused.

In his words, there is a strong here-and-now orientation to his perception of stress. This type of orientation is common; when stress is experienced, uncomfortable symptoms tend to accompany it. These symptoms compel the pilot to resolve the discomfort as soon as possible. A list of several common symptoms of stress is presented in Table 1–1. As you review this list, note which symptoms you have experienced over the past year and which ones you are currently experiencing, if any.

Another common observation I have made is that when stress is recognized, its symptoms are often minimized by the pilot:

> Sure I smoke heavily. It seems that the harder I work, the more I smoke. It's nothing but a bad habit—and besides, I enjoy it.

The pilot's minimization and resulting lack of acknowledgment of his own stress symptoms is one of the

Table 1–1
Indications of Stress

- Insomnia
- Trembling, weakness
- Grinding of the teeth (bruxism)
- Attention becomes fixated
- Tendency to overlook things
- Inclination to become fatigued
- Stuttering and difficulty with speech
- Difficulty remembering important information
- Recurring intrusive thoughts
- Nightmares
- Impulsive behavior
- Increased smoking or overeating
- Inability to concentrate
- Hyperalertness
- Emotional or physical isolation from others

- Diarrhea, indigestion
- Loss of appetite
- Frequent need to urinate
- Sweating
- Pounding of the heart
- Tendency to be highly emotional
- Emotional tension
- Easily excited
- Anxiety
- Alcohol or drug addiction
- Migraine headaches
- Confusion
- Neck pain
- Chronically tense muscles
- Proneness to accidents
- Increased self-doubt
- Cry for no reason
- Irritable
- Easily startled
- Depression

---

most dangerous traps. Unmanaged stress tends to increase progressively. The pilot needs greater knowledge of stress and its effects, and greater self-awareness of his involvement with stress to avoid this trap.

STRESS DEFINED

Webster's New World Dictionary defines stress, as it applies to humans, as:

> Stress: a) Mental or physical tension or strain;
> b) Urgency, pressure, etc. which causes this. . . .

As a general definition of stress, *Webster's* may be considered adequate. However, it does not provide a conceptualization of the unique experience of stress for the pilot. Stress must be understood beyond the simple parameters of "tension" or "strain," as these parameters are limited in their usefulness in determining why and how stress affects pilots. Because of this, a more specific definition is in order:

> Pilot Stress: An unresolved pressure, strain or force, acting upon the pilot's mental and physical systems which, if continued, will cause damage to those systems.

A thorough analysis of this definition will provide us with a better understanding of the role that stress plays in Pilot Stress Syndrome.

First, pressure is exerted when something is pressing or is being pressed, compressed, or squeezed. Pressures may affect the pilot mentally, as when the situation demands immediate decisions, or physically, when climbs and descents cause pressure changes in the inner ear. Time pressures, as most pilots are aware, also tend to be a common factor found in many pilot-induced aviation accidents and incidents.

To strain means to stretch or force beyond the normal limits. Most pilots are well aware of the effects of stress on the structural integrity of the airplane. Should normal operating limits be exceeded, the airplane may suffer structural damage. It is also true that excessive strain experienced by the pilot may lead to damage to the pilot's healthy mental and physical functioning. For instance, it has been demonstrated in the laboratory that when too much sensory information (information received through the sensations of sight, sound, touch, taste, and smell) is presented to the pilot in a given time frame, optimal levels of mental processing may be exceeded. Simply stated, the pilot can handle only a given amount of information at any particular time. If, for example, while flying, you are to receive more than two instructions from air traffic control simultaneously, you may find yourself hard-pressed to remember what the controller told you to do, making it impossible to carry out the controller's instructions. The human brain functions much like a computer. When it receives too much input it becomes overloaded and shuts down. Additionally, mental strain may make it quite difficult to make complex or rapid decisions, while the physical strain of fatigue may greatly affect your ability to perform physical tasks necessary for flight.

A "force" is some power or strength exerted against something else. Just as forces are necessary for the basic elements of flight—lift, weight, thrust, and drag—they are also necessary for normal mental and physical functioning. If any force is lacking, a counterforce acts upon the object. For instance, when the lift acting upon an aircraft decreases, the weight forces increase, resulting in a descent. The same principle applies to the pilot who experiences the forces of stress. This can be demonstrated by notable changes in the pilot's emotional state. Feelings such as anger, frustration, depression, fear, may accompany physiological changes in the body such as blood pressure, blood sugar levels, and oxygen levels in the blood. As one pilot put it:

I noticed that I was becoming extremely edgy and irritable. It didn't take very much to set me off. This went on for a month, until I finally went to see a doctor. He put me on blood pressure medication and since then I've been feeling fine.

The reverse may also occur, whereby physical changes in the body may accompany emotional changes:

> At first Don's illness didn't affect my work. But as he got worse, I found myself worrying constantly. Before I knew it, I was unable to eat. A pain in my stomach developed, and I was later diagnosed as having an ulcer. Needless to say, I had to take time off from the job.

Our definition of Pilot Stress states that pressures, strains, and forces act upon the pilot's "mental and physical systems." Though it is implied that these two systems operate independently of each other, this is actually not the case. These systems are both interactive and inseparable. Neither operates without influencing, or being influenced by, the other. This definition merely separates the mental from the physical system for the purpose of providing a clear understanding of the mental and physical aspects of the pilot as a functioning person. This will become more clear to you as we proceed.

GENERAL ADAPTATION SYNDROME

To further enlighten you on the subject of stress, I would like to draw upon a stress theory proposed by Hans Selye,[1] the father of modern stress research. His theory described the ways in which continued exposure to pressures, strains, and forces affect living organisms—human beings included. This theory can easily be applied to the effects of stress on pilots. He called his theory the "General Adaptation Syndrome."

According to this theory, all living organisms have a finite amount of adaptation energy which can be applied to chronic exposure to stress. "Adaptation energy" is

[1]Selye, H. (1974) *Stress Without Distress*. New York: Harper & Row.

Figure 1-1
General Adaptation Syndrome (GAS)

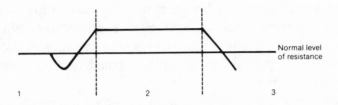

Source: Selye. H. (1974) *Stress Without Distress* (p. 27) New York: Harper & Row.

defined as the energy an organism possesses in order to acquire and maintain physical adaptation when faced with stressors.

The General Adaptation Syndrome occurs in three phases (see Figure 1–1).

1. Alarm Reaction Stage. This is characterized by the release of hormones in the body due to exposure to one or more stressors. During this phase the organism's resistance is low, so it is vulnerable to damage, illness, or even death, depending on the strength of the stressor or stressors presented. The symptoms of stress will be present during this phase (see Table 1–1).

2. Stage of Resistance. During this phase the organism recovers from the stressor(s) and attempts to cope. It is said that adaptation occurs during this phase. The symptoms that were present in the previous phase disappear and resistance is higher than normal.

3. Stage of Exhaustion. If stress persists, the third phase presents itself. The symptoms that were present during the Alarm Reaction Stage reappear, but cannot be reversed because the organism can no longer secrete the necessary amount of adrenal hormones, preventing the organism from physiologically coping with the stress. This results in the death of the organism.

Selye's theory provides us with an excellent model for

understanding the path that stress tends to take. When a pilot experiences stress, he can only handle the stress for a period of time before it takes its toll on his body. For instance, cardiovascular disease, a condition which is highly prevalent among people who live very stressful lives, is the primary cause for loss of medical certification among airmen.

Adaptation is the goal of all stress management. The longer you are able to adapt to stress, the longer you will live, and the better you will function in the cockpit. Those who adapt poorly experience the negative effects of stress more severely. We must be careful here, however; the adaptation that we are interested in maintaining involves more than the disappearance of stress symptoms. This can occur as the negative effects of stress continue. Instead, we are more concerned with taking steps to adapt by reducing the stressors in our personal and professional lives and by protecting ourselves from the negative effects of stress. It must be pointed out that Selye's interest was in the area of the body—the physical system. His theory did not address the mental system, which is of equal concern to pilots.

PSYCHOLOGICAL REACTION PATTERN

I have personally observed a psychological reaction pattern that pilots exhibit when experiencing stress that parallels Selye's physiologically oriented theory. This pattern also occurs in three phases.

First, when the pilot is exposed to high levels of stress, a marked decrease in coping ability may be observed. During this phase, it is common for the pilot to become short-tempered, confused, frustrated, or irrational. These emotional reactions are often magnified when the pilot is presented with demands made upon him—demands that would not normally evoke such intense reactions. The response of the pilot to demands is one which would be present for anyone whose capacity to respond in a flexible and adaptive manner is greatly diminished. A Learjet captain told me about his experience with this psychological phase of the stress pattern that resembles Selye's Alarm Reaction Stage:

> I love to fly the Lear 25. It's fast, it has power, it's comfortable, and I'm able to enjoy the same feeling that I experienced in the military while flying TAC missions. This, along with the fact that I've been able to fly scheduled passenger runs for the past year, has made my job great. Well, that all ended when we lost our major corporate contract. Then it was back to the hassle of an unpredictable schedule, and passengers who didn't appreciate a courteous and well-trained flight crew. On top of all of this, I lost my copilot. He went to the airlines. Then I had to break in a new guy who knew the airplane pretty well, but had no class. We started arguing about everything. After a month of this, I was a basket-case. That's why I'm here on a beach in Mexico for some good old-fashioned R and R. It beats jumping out of my skin every time somebody looks at me cross-eyed.

This pilot had to take a vacation to get away from the heavy demands of his job, which brought too many changes in a short period of time—more changes than he could handle. Of course, for him this was the beginning of his adaptation to the stressors that faced him.

The next psychological phase is marked by adjustment to the demands of the stressful situation. As with Selye's Stage of Resistance, the pilot's coping ability during this phase is at a high level. The pilot may exhibit command, confidence, and capability during this phase. I spoke with the same Learjet captain one month after he had returned to his job. He appeared confident and happy with his job:

> Things are going well. My stint on the beach was what I needed to sort things out. When I got back from Mexico, I sat down with the boss and told him what I would need to be happy here. Thank God I have some clout around this place. He listened and changes were made. I got myself a new copilot—one whom I selected. I asked for a raise and got it, and I have the marketing department working on getting us another scheduled service contract. At least I feel more in control.

Had the pilot not taken steps to actively reduce his stress, he would have eventually experienced the third phase of the psychological response pattern. This phase accompanies prolonged exposure to stress. At some point the pilot can no longer resist his stress. When this occurs, it may lead to psychological reactions, such as depression, feelings of helplessness, emotional withdrawal, heavy confusion, inability to focus one's thoughts, alcoholism, drug addiction, or other problems. For many pilots, this phase of adjustment results in loss of interest in flying and occupational burnout. As with Selye's Stage of Exhaustion, irreversible damage may occur, eventually leading to death. In this case the death would be psychological. Loss of interest in aviation and job burnout can be viewed as death of a career. For many pilots, this form of death creates an identity crisis. More important, it may affect safety in the cockpit.

Syndrome Defined

When I first observed stress reactions among pilots, I was unaware of an existing pattern of responses. All I knew was that pilots tended to be affected by stress in ways that were both similar and dissimilar to nonflyers.

My curiosity led me to ask myself two vital questions:

1. What types of stressors most adversely affect pilots?
2. How do these stressors affect pilots?

The answers caused a shift in my perspective of pilot stress.

I sought out patterns among the stressors that pilots experience and the patterned responses that are typical among pilots. I found that stress among pilots can most appropriately be viewed as a syndrome—a number of symptoms occurring together and characterizing a specific disease or condition.

THE TEN CATEGORIES
OF STRESS FACTORS

After much investigation, I found that ten categories of stress factors exist for the pilot. Each category is comprised of numerous related stressors. These categories, along with each of their related stressors, comprise the underlying factors that are both cause and effect elements of Pilot Stress Syndrome. The ten categories are:

1. *Conscious factors*—These factors relate to the pilot's conscious thought processes. These include thinking, perception, learning, concentration, information processing, judgment, workload, and decision making.

2. *Unconscious factors*—Many of the same processes used in conscious thinking are used in unconscious thinking. Other unconscious factors include memory storage of past experiences and the pilot's underlying motivations.

3. *Personality factors*—The pilot's personality plays a key role in pilot stress. It determines the pilot's atti-

tude toward stress and stressful events. It also influences the manner in which the pilot copes with stress, and can be an important determining factor in accident proneness.

4. *Psychological factors*—The pilot's psychological state can increase or decrease vulnerability to stress. When the pilot's mental state is positive, he can generally tolerate higher levels of stress. But when it is less positive, stress can take its toll. Some of the factors that affect the pilot's mental state are illness, fear, and anxiety.

5. *Physiological factors*—The pilot's physiological state is of major concern for safe flight. It is also vulnerable to the effects of stress.

6. *Environmental factors*—The environment in which the pilot works and lives can influence stress. Such factors as temperature, noise levels, comfort, and the climate of interaction with others are important environmental considerations.

7. *Experiential factors*—A pilot experiences flight and flight-related activities as no other person can. His perceptions, experiences, and even the language that he uses to convey these personal experiences to other pilots tend to be stressors in and of themselves.

8. *Sociocultural factors*—Professional aviation cannot exist without influencing and being influenced by the society in which it operates. Factors which are of sociocultural importance to the pilot can be highly stressful. They include economic factors, laws and regulations, industry trends and changes, current business and management practices, available technology, political factors, and the impact of airline deregulation.

9. *Life-change factors*—Changes in the pilot's personal and professional life can bring about stress. Some of these life-change factors include marriage, birth of a child, job change, and death of a parent.

10. *Acute reactive factors*—An acute reactive situation

may be defined as any situation requiring immediate corrective action. This corrective action may be necessary to prevent damage to persons or property. In some cases, it may be necessary to prevent the worsening of damage that has already occurred. Emergencies are acute reactive situations that pilots constantly prepare for. What most pilots are not prepared to deal with however, are stressful events such as occupational crises (being laid off, fired, or receiving a major cut in pay); personal-life crises (such as sudden illness in the family or economic problems); and normal versus abnormal resolution of stress resulting from an emergency.

These ten categories of stress-related factors are made up of stressors that are in many ways unique to pilots. Alone, no one category necessarily exists as a threat. As the number of stressors increase, however, safety risk also increases. Perhaps the most important thing for the pilot to understand is that stressors tend to interact cumulatively and synergistically. This means that as the effects of stress increase, they reach a point at which the total effect is greater than the sum of its parts—that is, $1 + 1 = 3$. The combined effects of the stressors on the pilot's mental and physical functioning increase geometrically, causing him to become overwhelmed by his stress. This may lead to mental and/or physical impairment. Mental impairment affects the pilot's thinking, planning, analyzing, decision making, problem solving, memory, and recall abilities. Physical impairment affects the pilot's ability to effectively maintain coordination, or to carry out tasks necessary for safe flight.

This leads to the definition of the syndrome that I have been describing:

Pilot Stress Syndrome: A stress syndrome affecting pilots that is brought about by exposure to stressors which are unique to pilots. These stressors interact cumulatively and synergistically to cause a breakdown in normal mental and physical functioning.

2

Characteristics of Pilot Stress

Adaptation. This simple word says it all. Pilots who are able to meet the demands of personal and occupational life stressors are generally happier and tend to live more fulfilling lives. They are also safer in the cockpit.

Selye's theory showed us that adaptation energy is finite. This means that the pilot has to contend with the problem of conserving this limited resource to prevent its rapid depletion. The goal, then, is to extend the duration of adaptation through techniques, strategies, and practices that will increase the pilot's flexibility and adaptability toward stressful situations. Such a task calls for an awareness of the ways in which adaptive energy can be maximized. The maximization of adaptive energy is important for two reasons: First, optimal functioning in the cockpit is a must for safe flight. When stress levels are high, pilots tend to refocus their mental and physical energies away from flight-related thoughts and activities. A regional airline first officer's words clearly illustrate the problem that this can create:

We were on the initial approach segment of our flight. The tension had been there [in the cockpit] all along. My mind kept drifting and I was behind the airplane. It was a good thing the captain knew what I was going through—with the wife leaving, and all that. He worked a lot harder than usual—I know he did, but my mind wasn't moving as fast as the airplane was.

Secondly, adaptive energy must be available at those times when the pilot needs it most. These periods include the times when emergency situations are encountered, major life transitions are taking place, and when the pilot is engaged in the critical phases of flight when mental and physical functioning are at peak demand.

As we explore each of the categories of stress factors that comprise Pilot Stress Syndrome, it will be important for you to understand and consider the dynamics that interplay to provide the stressors with their destructive potential. These dynamic factors are simple—perhaps so simple that they have been overlooked by experts in the aviation field. But simplicity doesn't equate to harmlessness. Most of the errors that are made in aircraft cockpits are not very complex, but their effects are at times devastating. Serious consideration is in order here.

When I was finally able to determine what individual stressors tended to affect pilots, I had a feeling that there had to be more to it than just stressors affecting pilots. There had to be something that was inherent in the stressors themselves. Otherwise, stress wouldn't have the negative impact that it often has on pilots. Closer examination revealed the characteristics that can act alone, or interact, to provide stress with its ability to escalate to the point in which its effects can reach dangerous levels. Some of these characteristics are directly related to the stressors, and some are indirectly related, affecting the pilot's receptivity to stress effects. These characteristics are:

- Intensity of the stressor
- Quality of the stressor
- Duration and frequency of exposure to the stressor
- Focus of the stressor
- Extensity of the stressor's effects
- The pilot's mental and physical condition
- The pilot's ability to resist stress
- The pilot's perception of the stressor and its potential effects

These characteristics are also responsible for increasing and decreasing the duration of adaptation.

INTENSITY OF THE STRESSOR

The intensity of a stressor is its magnitude. When considering the effects of a stressor's intensity on the pilot's physical system, we are interested in knowing if the stressor is too strong, too loud, too bright, or if it creates too much physical pain or pressure for the pilot to adapt to.

To understand how the concept of intensity applies to the pilot's mental system, we must look closely at the pilot's behavior. In particular, we must concern ourselves with the magnitude of the response that the stressor evokes. If we observe that the pilot is overreacting to a stressor, we can assume that the stressor is of high intensity. If, on the other hand, there is little or no emotional response to a stressor, its intensity may be considered to be low. A flight engineer student told of his response to an overly demanding simulator instructor:

> My simulator instructor was on my case all afternoon. It was a frustrating day for both of us. I just wasn't

understanding the electrical system at all. Every time I made a mistake he yelled louder. It was getting to me. The louder he yelled, the angrier I got. I finally reached the point where I couldn't take it any longer, and I started yelling back at him. I must have been pretty loud myself, because when I looked over my right shoulder, I noticed that a crowd had gathered at the entrance of the simulator.

This pilot's response was exaggerated. He and everybody within hearing distance knew it. Had he not reacted to the high-intensity stressor—his simulator instructor's unreasonable demands—he might have responded in a calmer manner.

QUALITY OF THE STRESSOR

The quality of a stressor is its nature or specific characteristics. Two important components of a stressor's quality are the source of the stressor and the identification of the specific elements that help to define it as a "stressor."

Stress can have as its source one or more stressors. When the pilot is negatively affected by stress, each stressor must be identified before effective stress management can take place.

Once the stressor has been identified, its specific characteristics should be determined. This is accomplished through close examination of the stressful object, event, or situation. By taking a close look at the stressor, the pilot can identify such features as its size, shape, magnitude, potential for threat, and its significance to the pilot. Knowledge of a stressor's characteristics, along with awareness of the dynamics of pilot stress, will aid in protection from the detrimental effects that the stressor can inflict upon the pilot.

DURATION AND FREQUENCY OF EXPOSURE TO THE STRESSOR

Duration and frequency are the time-related components of a stressor. A stressor's duration refers to its persistence over time, while a stressor's frequency refers to the number of times that it is experienced over a given period of time. When concerned with a stressor's duration, we are interested in knowing how long the pilot has been exposed to the stressor. In considering the frequency of exposure to a stressor, we are concerned with knowing how often the pilot has been exposed.

The concepts of duration and frequency, as they apply to exposure to stressors, are also closely linked to the concept of intensity (magnitude). When the duration of a high-intensity stressor is short, its effects may be physically and/or mentally detrimental to the pilot. This type of exposure is usually obvious to the pilot. However, when a stressor's intensity is low, its duration may continue to the point of causing serious physical and/or mental damage. This latter case is often more damaging because pilots tend to "put up" with lower-intensity stressors for longer periods of time before taking corrective action, if any is to be taken at all. Stressors that are of high intensity may also be experienced frequently enough to cause damage, the same holding true for low-intensity stressors. Once again, the latter of the two may present more severe problems over a period of time, as this condition may also go unchecked.

FOCUS OF THE STRESSOR

The focus of a stressor refers to its ability to locate itself in an area that is most vulnerable to the pilot. Unlike a stressor's quality (which is the nature or characteristic of the stressor itself), a stressor's focus relates to the receiver's (pilot's) vulnerabilities. These are the "soft spots" that the pilot possesses. A DC-8 captain addressed one area where he was most vulnerable to stress:

> The particular run that I'll be taking on Sunday will take us into Hartfield Airport. It doesn't seem to bother a lot of the other pilots, but I have this thing about Atlanta—I get these funny vibes. I feel so uptight about it that I've requested a transfer.

This pilot's stressor was his need to fly into Hartfield Airport despite the anticipatory anxiety that it evoked. The focus of the stressor for this pilot was embedded in his discomfort with flying into this particular airport. I later discovered that his discomfort was actually caused by unresolved fear resulting from a near-miss that he had experienced several years before, shortly after departing Hartfield Airport. Once this was revealed, the focus of the stressor was assigned to his unresolved fear. This was the area where he was most vulnerable to the stressor.

A stressor may be directed toward the pilot in one of two ways: intentionally or unintentionally. The former is directed through an attack or threat made by another person, or through the intentional assignment of tasks —as by a boss or senior crewmember—which are known to be stressful to the pilot. Unintentionally directed stress differs in that it is randomly directed. It is not purposely aimed at the pilot. Whether intentionally or unintentionally directed, the pilot must take steps to reduce his vulnerability to these types of stressors. The pilot does not have to be a victim of stressors. You will learn how to do this as you proceed.

EXTENSITY OF THE STRESSOR'S EFFECTS

Extensity of a stressor refers to its scope of influence. When we are concerned with a stressor's extensity, we are interested in knowing the extent to which it is affecting the pilot's life. Is it affecting his personal life? Social life? Professional life? And in what specific areas is it affecting each of these? We want to know what effect the stressor is having on the pilot and how far-reaching it is. A corporate pilot I interviewed spoke of his stress, which was quite extensive:

> The stress that I experienced affected virtually every area of my life. I couldn't do anything without thinking about the possibility of losing the entire corporate flight department. Things weren't going too well for the company financially, and unless something miraculous were to happen, I knew that I, along with the flight department, would be the first to go—after all, the jet was a luxury that was rapidly becoming a burden. My wife, my kids, and my friends had to wait until the crisis was over before I could be myself with them again.

When a stressor is too extensive it may affect every area of the pilot's life, as in the above example. The greater a stressor's extensity, the more it will adversely affect the duration of adaptation.

THE PILOT'S MENTAL AND PHYSICAL CONDITION

The pilot's mental and physical status are also variables that will affect the duration of adaptation. When he is both mentally and physically healthy, adaptation will endure for longer periods of time. Healthier pilots tend to be more flexible and adaptable to a wider range of stressors. When the pilot is not mentally and/or physically healthy, vulnerability to stress increases. This may significantly reduce the duration of adaptation for the pilot.

THE PILOT'S ABILITY TO RESIST STRESS

The fact remains that all pilots react to stressors differently—their stress responses are in many ways idiosyncratic. The fact also remains that a pilot may go on, seemingly forever, adapting to high-intensity stressors (or even low-intensity stressors, for that matter), until one day he can no longer adapt. If this failure to adapt comes about suddenly and unexpectedly in the cockpit, it may result in a fatal error. The belief that stress will not take its toll on you because you seem to handle it well is another one of those traps that pilots fall into. Remember, no pilot is immune to Pilot Stress Syndrome. The highest level of stress tolerance that any pilot should consider himself possessing is that of active management status, as opposed to low stress-tolerance. By active management, I mean that the pilot is actively engaged in a structured daily program of stress management. This does not prevent all stress from being experienced, but it does maximize tolerance to stress. The least tolerant state is that which I call the "low stress-tolerance" state.

THE PILOT'S PERCEPTION
OF THE STRESSOR
AND ITS POTENTIAL EFFECTS

Perception—the way we experience and interpret information both internally, through thoughts, emotions, and physical sensations, and externally, from our environment, can have an impact on stress. The way we perceive is influenced by the experiences we have had in life. When the pilot encounters a stressor, it will be interpreted according to similar objects, events, or situations encountered at some time in the pilot's past. These could include both recent and early life experiences. If the stressor is closely associated with a highly stressful object, event, or situation, the pilot might perceive it as a physical or psychological threat. Whether the threat is real or imagined, stress can increase; imagined threats are very real to the pilot, as with all humans. Should the stressor be perceived as less threatening, its effects may be less serious.

While the pilot's perceptions are important, they are not the only determining factor for risk of dangerous stress effects. All of the characteristics presented here and how they interact must be considered.

INTERACTIONAL EFFECTS

In most cases no single stressor causes a breakdown in the pilot's ability to function. It is when the stressor's intensity is very high, or when the various pilot/stressor characteristics (intensity, quality, duration/frequency, extensity, etc.) interact in harmful ways, that the pilot may become negatively affected. These harmful interactional effects will become more clear as we examine three stress profiles that pilots exhibit.

The eight pilot/stress characteristics are:

1. Intensity (In)   —Magnitude
2. Quality (Q)   —Nature, characteristics
3. Duration/Frequency   —Exposure over time/
   (D/F)   Number of occurrences
                           in a given time period

4. Focus of Stressor   —Stressor's ability to zero
   (F)   in on pilot's vulnerable
                             areas
5. Extensity (E)   —Scope of influence
6. Mental/Physical   —Status of mental/
   Status (M/P)   physical condition
7. Resistance (R)   —Pilot's ability to resist
                             stress
8. Perception (P)   —Interpretation

Each of these characteristics can be presented in terms of their stress effects, ranging from least serious to most serious:

In   – Low <– – –> High
Q   – Insignificant <– – –> Very significant
D/F   – Short exposure <– – –> Long exposure
         Infrequent exposure <– – –> Frequent
         exposure
F   – Vulnerable <– – –> Highly vulnerable
E   – Isolated <– – –> Quite extensive
M/P   – Excellent mental condition <– – –> Poor
         mental condition
         Excellent physical condition <– – –>
         Poor physical condition
R   – Actively managing stress <– – –> Not
         actively managing stress
P   – Perceptions don't intensify stress effects
         <– – –> Perceptions dramatically
         intensify stress effects

These ranges comprise a scale that can be used to describe various stress profiles. I call this scale the Stress Dynamics Scale. The most serious stress profile, as illustrated by the Stress Dynamics Scale, is as follows:

In   – High
Q   – Very significant

D/F   –   Long exposure/Frequent exposure
F   –   Highly vulnerable
E   –   Quite extensive
M/P   –   Poor mental condition/Poor physical
            condition
R   –   Not actively managing stress
P   –   Perceptions dramatically intensify stress
            effects

In this profile each of the characteristics show serious stress effects. I call this the Nonfunctioning Stress Profile (NSP) because the pilot who possesses such a profile is not capable of functioning without serious mental and/or physical impairment. As each of these characteristics show stress in terms of their maximum range, we may assume that the sum total of their interaction will result in high stress-levels.

Conversely, the least serious stress profile will show minimal stress effects on the Stress Dynamics Scale:

In   –   Low
Q   –   Insignificant
D/F   –   Short exposure/Infrequent exposure
F   –   Vulnerable
E   –   Isolated
M/P   –   Excellent mental condition/Excellent
            physical condition
R   –   Actively managing stress
P   –   Perceptions don't intensify stress

A pilot whose stress profile resembles this is capable of functioning without being affected detrimentally by stress—so long as his stress profile does not change. I call this the Maximum Functioning Stress Profile (MFSP).

But what about the pilot who doesn't fit either the NSP or the MFSP? This is not uncommon. In fact, most pilots don't exhibit either of these profiles. Instead, they may show maximum range in relation to only one area on the Stress Dynamics Scale, while experiencing minimum to medium range levels in each of the other areas. The effect of a single stressor that lies within the maximum range along a single area of the scale may or may not result in adverse stress effects on the pilot. But rather than denying the possibility of negative stress effects, it would be safer to assume that the pilot will be at risk. Hence, a pilot who should be considered to be "at risk" might possess a stress profile that appears as follows:

In   –   Low
Q   –   Significant
D/F   –   Short exposure/Infrequent exposure
F   –   Vulnerable
E   –   Isolated
M/P   –   Excellent mental condition/Excellent physical condition
R   –   Actively managing stress
P   –   Perceptions don't intensify stress

All of these characteristics appear to support the MFSP profile except one. In this example, it is the quality (Q) of the stressor that puts the pilot at risk, because it is at the maximum (serious) range along the scale.

It is not known exactly how many stress characteristics must be experienced at the maximum level before the pilot's overall stress level should be considered serious. For one pilot, it may require five stress characteristics. For another pilot, only one may be necessary. And still, for the same pilot it may vary at different times—two at one time, six at another.

At present there are no objective methods available that can be used to predict the exact number of stress characteristics which must be affected in order to reach the stress levels that are considered dangerous to the pilot. Because of this, it would be appropriate to take a conservative stance and assume that anytime a pilot rates himself in the maximum range with respect to any single stress characteristic, he should consider himself at risk and take the necessary steps to manage his stress. We will use the Stress Dynamics Scale later in this book as an assessment tool to help you become aware of the specific areas in which stress may be affecting your personal or professional life.

POSITIVE VERSUS NEGATIVE STRESS

I have frequently referred to the phrase "negative stress." I feel that this needs clarification. Most pilots associate stress with negative events: bad weather, low fuel, a demanding flight schedule. What most of us fail to realize is that stress is not always negative. In fact, we

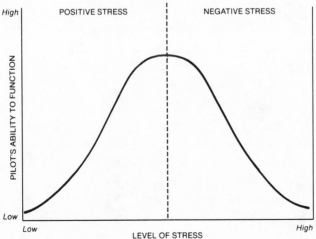

Figure 2-1
Positive and Negative Stress

can't survive without it. Some degree of stress must be present at all times. When we sleep, our nervous system continues to function. This causes stress. When we fly we must be aware of our surroundings. The alertness that is required for this awareness causes stress. Living and breathing are not stress-free. Life and stress are synonymous. One cannot exist without the other. In Figure 2–1 we can see that the pilot's ability to function is dependent on stress.

When the pilot is functioning positively, he is experiencing positive stress. But there is a point at which increased stress will cause him to become less functional. As the stress continues to increase, the pilot becomes less able to function mentally and physically. When this occurs, he is experiencing the negative effects of stress.

3

Conscious and Unconscious Factors

Awareness is the first step in managing pilot stress. The pilot who is keenly aware of his abilities and limitations and the capabilities and limits of the aircraft he flies is better prepared to maintain control when stressful situations arise.

The importance of awareness is not just limited to the abilities, capabilities, and limitations of the pilot and his aircraft, however. For stress to be managed effectively, the pilot must also be aware of all available information pertinent to the safe operation of the flight. FARs, en route and destination weather, traffic information, fuel status, location of the aircraft relative to the navaids, and instrument indications represent only a partial list of the many things of which the pilot must be aware. Such vast awareness can only come about through the process of thinking.

THINKING

The ability to think intelligently is what sets humans apart from lower forms of life. For the pilot, thought is his primary tool of survival, both on the ground and in the air.

When one thinks about thinking (it's rather amazing that we can do this) it becomes obvious that thinking is a process which is actually very complex. As you continue to read about the activities involved in the thinking process, bear in mind that each aspect of this process contains its own unique stressors.

CONSCIOUS THOUGHT

Thinking occurs on two levels: conscious and unconscious. Conscious thinking involves thought that exists within the scope of the pilot's immediate awareness.

Two major problems that develop out of conscious thinking that tend to produce stress are persistent, recurring thoughts and overload. Recurring thoughts tend to remain in the forefront of the pilot's consciousness, often preventing him from attending to important flight-related tasks. A previous argument, financial troubles, fears, and pressure to meet a demanding schedule are some of the popular causes for the pilot's persistent, recurring thoughts. The common factor in each case is that the problem causing the recurring thought is unresolved. If these thoughts keep the pilot from sleeping at night, fatigue sets in. This increases the pilot's stress level. As the problem worsens, he finds it difficult to function normally on the job. This further increases stress. Fortunately, there is a way to deal with recurring thoughts: that is simply to work toward the resolution of the problems leading to them. As resolution comes about, these thoughts tend to become less frequent and intense. Pilots who avoid facing their problems are more prone to experiencing this problem.

Overload, the other major stress-producing problem related to conscious thinking, results from the need to process too much information at one time (recall the computer example in Chapter 2). When we are overloaded we may find ourselves forgetting important information, overlooking things (such as routine checklist items), feeling helpless, and perhaps frustrated and angry. At times, a pilot may even feel hopeless. When this occurs, he usually feels stuck and unable to do anything right. This pilot may simply give up because nothing he does seems to work. The other flight crewmembers will usually find this pilot's experience of hopelessness stressful, because the hopeless pilot will typically abandon some, if not all, of his duties, increasing the workload for the remaining crewmembers.

UNCONSCIOUS THINKING

Unconscious thinking occurs outside the realm of the pilot's conscious awareness. Unlike conscious thought, unconscious thought processes are busy at work twenty-four hours per day. While awake and asleep, we unconsciously interpret information that we acquire from the environment so that our actions will help us to survive. There are several functions that unconscious thinking serves for the pilot. These include memory storage, identity protection, overload protection, and problem solving.

Memory storage is important to the pilot because it allows him to draw upon his past experiences to meet the demands of the challenges that face him in the present. Everything that happens to us in our lives becomes recorded as unconscious memories. When events occur in the present which are similar to past events, we unconsciously compare the past and present information in order to determine the most favorable way to handle the present situation.

Identity protection is the second important function of the unconscious thought processes. The pilot's identity consists of his perception of who he is, his likes and dislikes, his beliefs, and his perception of how others perceive him. Unconscious thought processes strongly serve to maintain the pilot's identity by resisting change. Change is usually perceived as a threat to the identity, for when change occurs, the pilot must act differently. Acting differently is often very stressful to the pilot because it forces him to reevaluate his beliefs about who he is—a process that may prove to be both lengthy and uncomfortable. Because it is easier not to change, and because lack of change tends to make life more predictable, resistance to change is typically the norm among pilots. Just as stress may come about with change, it can often be greater when change does not take place. This is particularly true when the pilot's identity fosters stressful behavior. The "Type A" behavior of many pilots is a good example. The pilot who engages in this form of behavior is typically highly driven, motivated, aggressive, and is characterized as a "workaholic" (see Chapter 4).

Because the pilot can attend to only one or two tasks at a time, overload protection must be present to protect him from ignoring other relevant tasks. This is becoming more important now than it was in the earlier days of flight, as pilots are moving further away from the hands-on control of their aircraft, toward that of monitoring modern automated aircraft control systems. The well-trained and experienced pilot depends greatly upon his ability to unconsciously monitor and interpret his activities and the progress of flight, so that he can consciously attend to the important task of flying his aircraft. The overload protection function of unconscious thought processes can become a source of stress when the pilot possesses inadequate knowledge of, or only partial information regarding, the item or situation being monitored.

The fourth function to consider is that of unconscious problem solving, which incorporates the activities of the three prior functions already mentioned. In order for the pilot to solve problems effectively, he must unconsciously compare past and present events (memory storage function); evaluate his identity considerations (identity protection function); and gather as much information as possible about the current problem (overload protection function). Once each of these steps has been taken, the information is analyzed and tentative alternative solutions are derived. The pilot then unconsciously chooses the solution that will align most with his unconscious needs and motivations.

Stress presents itself when the solution selected fails to solve the problem at hand. If the problem worsens because of a faulty solution, stress will usually increase more rapidly. Pilots are often caught between a rock and a hard place because they are expected to take steps that are appropriate to solve inflight problems, but there are times when the solution may not be so clear.

This is illustrated well by a 727 captain's explanation of how he had to fly using nonstandard procedures to land his fully loaded aircraft safely when caught in a thunderstorm.

I was on a flight from Portland to Denver. The airplane was fully loaded and we had taken on extra fuel because there were thunderstorms all along our route of flight. ATC had instructed us to take this route into

Denver based on weather reports they had received. It turned out that this particular route was not very good at all. We had descended to 15,000 feet. Upon arriving at that altitude we encountered severe turbulence. I requested 11,000. The controller came back and said, "You won't like it at 11,000 feet; it's really rough there." I knew that we had to get down and I didn't want to go back into what I had just come out of, so I asked for 11,000 again. The controller cleared to me 11,000. I used the speed brake to get down rapidly. With the power off, I found myself climbing at 4,000 feet per minute. I eventually got down to 11,000 feet. Then I immediately had to go to full power with the speed brake off because we caught wind shear. We went from 260 knots to 190 knots in 5 seconds. I got a stick-shaker. We then broke out of the clouds and were in the clear right over downtown Denver at 11,000 feet. I saw that we were way too high to land, but there was a thunderstorm sitting right at the end of the runway. We had to land, there was no choice. ATC could not approve a landing on runway eight right. They told me that we were cleared to land on eight left. The flight engineer, who had been silent, spoke up. He said we were too heavy. I thought about my options and instructed the crew that we were going to land anyway. I knew that we wouldn't be able to execute a missed approach because we'd have to fly into another storm. There was no place to go but to the airport. So I did something very unorthodox. I pulled the throttles all the way to idle and immediately went from 0° to 40° flaps without stopping at the gates, and flew the airplane to the runway. I was able to land and stop the airplane within the first half of the runway. Nine out of ten pilots would not have tried this, but I found it necessary to exercise my emergency authority as captain. I had no doubt that we'd make it because I had practiced and taught this procedure in the simulator for years. It was considered a nonstandard procedure because it was not published in the company manual.

This pilot did something that was not considered acceptable to his company, but his solution worked. He was obviously faced with a dilemma—to fly nonstandard and land the plane as he had only done in the simulator, or to continue on into a thunderstorm with known severe turbulence and wind-shear conditions. Had he crashed while executing either of his options, he would have been in the wrong. Instead he opted to use the nonstandard procedure. He felt that if he had followed company procedures, he would have been "dead right."

PERCEPTION

Perception tends to be an integral part of both the conscious and unconscious thinking processes. In its simplest definition, perception may be described as the way in which we view the world around us. When we perceive, we first internalize information from the environment via one or more of our five senses. We then compare that information (unconsciously and, at times, consciously) to see how it compares with objects, events, or situations that we have experienced in the past. If the association is strong enough between the past and present information, the pilot will act in a similar or different manner from that taken in the past, depending upon the outcome of his past actions.

No two pilots perceive the same object, event, or situation in the same manner. The FAA, the various branches of the military and air carriers, are aware of this fact. This has led to continued efforts in the aviation industry to minimize the problems that arise from perceptual discrepancies that tend to exist between flight crewmembers. The solution has been standardized flight crew training. By theory, this approach suggests that pilots who fly as flight crewmembers should be able to work effectively with pilots with whom they have never flown before. This is because all of the pilots are trained to follow the same procedures. While this approach is helpful, there are some perceptual problems that cannot be overcome by standardized training. These problems are inherent in the pilot's natural perceptual processes. We, as pilots, must be aware of them because they can lead to errors that can produce stress, and worse yet, they can be the source of fatal errors in the cockpit. These problems center around certain principles of perception.

The first of these perceptual principles is demonstrated in Figure 3–1. Two objects are presented that many pilots tend to perceive as a circle and a square. However, it may be argued that what is presented in these illustrations is not a circle and a square, but rather a series of lines. This phenomenon demonstrates the *principle of closure*, which reflects the pilot's tendency to fill in any existing gaps in his perception.

In flight, the pilot may have available to him only partial information related to such factors as en route or destination weather conditions, instructions from air traffic control, or the extent of an aircraft systems malfunction. Should the pilot misperceive the true situational status of any relevant information pertaining to the flight, the stage will be set for increased stress in the cockpit. This may come about through lack of information, misinformation, or ambiguous information. Any of these conditions can cause the pilot to wrongly fill in the existing informational gaps. This may mentally result in miscalculation, over- or underestimation, and faulty de-

Figure 3-1
Incomplete Figures

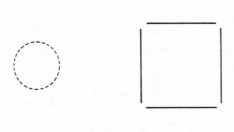

Source: Lundin. R. (1979) *Theories and Systems of Psychology* (2nd ed.) (p. 227) Lexington, MA: D.C. Heath and Company.

cision making; and may behaviorally result in continued flight into adverse weather conditions, continued flight with a less than airworthy airplane, and inadequate or inappropriate execution of normal, irregular, or emergency procedures.

Other perceptual principles that may affect the pilot (Figure 3–2) are the *principle of proximity* (elements which are close together tend to be perceived in groups);

Figure 3-2
Principles of Organization

Principle of Proximity

00   00   00   00

Principle of Objective Set

00   00   00   00   00000000

Principle of Similarity

XXX   000XXX000   XXX000XXX

Source: Wertheimer, M. (1979) "Principles of Organization." In R. Lundin, Ed., *Theories and Systems of Psychology* (2nd ed.) (pp. 226–227) Lexington, MA: D.C. Heath and Company.

the *principle of objective set* (if a series of objects or events is perceived that lead to a mental set, that mental set might continue to be perceived despite any changes that might occur); and the *principle of similarity* (similar objects or events tend to be perceived together).

It would be reasonable to assume that stress can magnify any of these perceptual manifestations.

LEARNING

Learning, defined by the FAA as a change in behavior as a result of experience, can have a strong influence on stress among pilots.

Proper training helps the pilot develop skills necessary for the safe and efficient handling of the aircraft. It also helps him cope with aviation-related stressors that are encountered throughout his flying career. As the pilot's experience and familiarity broaden, stress and anxiety tend to decrease, even in emergency situations. The pilot who becomes more adept at using his mental abilities while flying will thus have an increased capacity for coping with stress.

Problems occur, however, when the pilot encounters learning difficulties. Learning difficulties occurring at any point during his aviation career may result in negative transfer of learned material. This means that a task or procedure improperly learned in one situation may be improperly applied to another situation. A common example of negative transfer of learning can be seen among airline pilots who have gained their early flight experience as fighter pilots. Having learned to be self-sufficient and self-disciplined, it is often difficult for these pilots to adjust to good crew-coordination practices. Though self-sufficiency and self-discipline are necessary attributes for the fighter pilot, they may be viewed as improper learning for multicrew flight operations requiring each pilot to work as a member of a cockpit team.

If left unresolved, negative transfer will result in limited capabilities on the part of the pilot. Possessing less flexibility, the pilot may be more prone to stress when operating in the area of his deficiency.

CONCENTRATION

Through concentration the pilot becomes focused, enabling all aspects of the thinking process to be used more effectively. Concentration is desirable up to a point, after which fixation tends to set in. The technical term for fixation is "attentional channelization."

Studies of flight crew attentiveness have revealed several facts that every pilot should be aware of regarding this problem.

First, when the pilot experiences stress his awareness becomes heightened. This can be positive unless his attention becomes channelized on one item, causing him to ignore other important items.

Second, when one pilot's attention becomes channelized, the entire flight crew may also fixate on the same object or event. This leaves important flight-related tasks unattended—like flying the aircraft.

Third, when the entire flight crew becomes attentionally channelized, the crew's channelization may take place at the wrong time for too long a period of time.

Each of the above problems can be both stressful and dangerous. Anytime one or more flight crewmembers becomes attentionally channelized, it sets the stage for increased stress levels in the cockpit. Other crewmembers may be forced to work harder, or they too may channelize, leaving the aircraft mentally and operatively unattended. Should the flight crew be lucky and not crash the aircraft as a result, they might face the highly stressful task of catching up with an aircraft that has run away from them. There is nothing more stressful than an entire flight crew that is operationally behind the aircraft they are flying.

One other phenomenon worth mentioning is what I call "airborne hypnosis." This is a form of attentional channelization that results from monotonous sounds, lights, or objects. The tendency of the human brain is to focus on some particular thing when everything in the environment remains constant for long periods of time. I have personally interviewed pilots who have fallen asleep while at the controls of their aircraft. These occurrences typically take place at night, when the radio is silent, traffic is minimal, and the pilot is fatigued. The constant droning of the engines, the warm cockpit, and darkness in the windshield can lull the pilot to sleep. Before he realizes it, he awakens to a nightmare. He pinches himself and realizes that he's not dreaming. By God, he's in a real airplane! He doesn't know where he is, and worse yet, he doesn't know how long he's been sleeping. All he knows is that he is headed somewhere. Stress? You bet! Every pilot and every flight crew should be aware of this very real problem.

INFORMATION PROCESSING

Once the pilot receives information from the environment, he must decide what he should do with it. This requires careful mental processing of that information.

Information processing takes place in a three-phase sequence. First comes the input phase, where information is transmitted from the environment via one or more of the five senses to the brain. The input of information can be affected when stress is experienced by the pilot, because stress can cause him to be less receptive to environmental information. Another problem that may occur during this phase was mentioned earlier—the tendency for perceptual illusions to become magnified with stress.

During the second phase of information processing, the pilot will decide upon the action to be taken. This requires him to recognize, sort out, and categorize the various pieces of information that he will ultimately respond to. This is accomplished both consciously and unconsciously. After this sequence of tasks has taken place, the pilot will decide whether action should or should not be taken. Stress can inhibit successful information processing during this phase by interfering with the pilot's concentration and his ability to recall important information. Stress can also cause the pilot to become attentionally channelized, preventing him from attending to one or more important parts of the information processing sequence.

The third phase of information processing involves the pilot's response. Should he experience such stress-related symptoms as fatigue, agitation, physical weakness, or poor nourishment that often accompany stress, his ability to respond adequately will be hindered.

JUDGMENT

The act of judging involves comparing, deciding, estimating, and understanding. When the pilot engages in effective stress-management practices, he increases his likelihood of exercising good judgment. Several elements of good judgment are enhanced through stress management. They include:

- Positive mental attitude
- Mental and physical alertness
- Proper planning
- Awareness of the environment in which he is operating
- Memory recall
- Concentration
- Communication
- Professionalism
- Ability to assess matters realistically
- Ability to utilize available resources effectively
- Ability to interact effectively with others
- Flexibility and adaptability

Pilots who fail to manage their stress operate their aircraft with the diminished capacities that accompany stress. Failure to achieve acceptable performance, based on inability to adequately compare, decide, estimate, and understand, constitutes poor judgment—a condition that can and should be actively avoided by the pilot.

WORKLOAD

Workload in the cockpit can increase stress. As workload increases, the pilot must mentally adjust to meet situational demands. Should the demand for mental processing exceed his capacity to process information, the pilot will experience mental overload. This further increases stress.

When stress is experienced in the cockpit due to increased workload, it may not be equally shared by each flight crewmember. Scientific studies conducted to measure the effects of cockpit workload have revealed enlightening information about the ways in which pilots experience workload-related stress.

For the captain, the heaviest workload is attributed to flying the aircraft. Captains experience the greatest degree of mental effort and stress during takeoff and landing; while heart rate (a measure of workload) peaks during the landing segment of the flight. Airline captains may even experience a heart-rate increase of as much as 10% upon entering the cockpit. Some researchers attribute this to increased responsibility.

For the first officer, increased workload is generally attributed to communications with air traffic control, with the highest rate of radio interchange taking place during the takeoff and landing portions of a flight. The lowest level of communications workload occurs during the en route portion of the flight. The use of checklists and the handling of ATC clearances during the departure and approach segments of a flight are also a major source of workload for the first officer.

For both pilots, heart rate has been found to peak during preflight and takeoff segments; and fatigue increases as the flight progresses. With respect to fatigue, it is interesting to note that flight crewmembers experience greater amounts of fatigue during flights that terminate between 5:00 A.M. and 9:30 A.M., with fatigue being less during flights that terminate between 10:30 P.M. and 1:00 A.M. Also, heart rate measures for night-instrument approaches are about the same as approaches conducted during daylight hours.

Every pilot should be aware of the effects of workload on stress. With the predictable, and at times not so predictable, fluctuations in workload, come increased mental demands on each pilot. By knowing when stress tends to be greatest for each pilot, the cockpit crew is more able to coordinate their efforts to avoid the introduction of unnecessary stressors during critical high-stress phases of flight. One of my clients, a DC-9 first officer, used his knowledge of cockpit workload to help himself and his captain to fly under less stressful conditions:

> There are actions that are mandated by the company that must be carried out in the cockpit. But nobody says that we can't use good old-fashioned common sense. When I learned about the connection between workload and pilot stress, I sat down with the captain and we went through every phase of each flight that we have together. We were able to work out our own system for reducing the cockpit workload. Now we're working more efficiently and we're less fatigued at the end of our duty time. This was a breakthrough in stress management for both of us.

This pilot reported to me that he and the captain with whom he flies are reacting less to frustrated air traffic controllers, and are enjoying their work much more. Their knowledge and understanding of workload is helping them accomplish certain tasks at times during flight which causes them to experience less mental overload.

THE PILOT STRESS PROFILE

During periods when workload is greatest, the margin for errors made by pilots tends to be smallest. There are two reasons why this is so. First, when the pilots or flight crew are busy, time may lapse before an error is recognized. Second, the error may escalate to the point where its effects are serious before corrective action can be taken. A curve showing the relationship between workload and aircraft accidents is presented in Figure 3–3. Note that

Figure 3-3
Pilot Workload During Different Phases of Flight

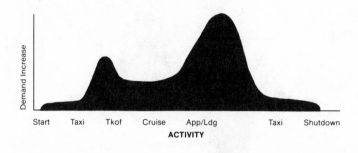

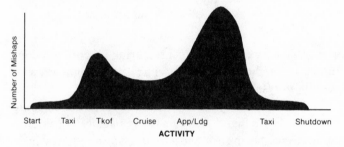

Source: Richardson, J. (1978) "CFIT: A Human Factors Problem." *Aerospace Safety,* 2, 3.

the critical phases of flight are represented by the higher workload demand regions on the graph. This graph represents the number of aircraft mishaps that tend to occur during each phase of flight.

In Figure 3–4 I have expanded the graph to represent a profile of pilot stress. This "Pilot Stress Profile" acknowledges a linear relationship between workload and stress in the cockpit.

A clear description of each phase of flight will illustrate the specific relationships that exist between workload and stress. These phases are:

1. *Anticipatory Phase*—Occurs from the point when the first engine starts to the point just prior to takeoff (right after completion of the taxi-out checklist).

Figure 3-4
Stress Dynamics Scale

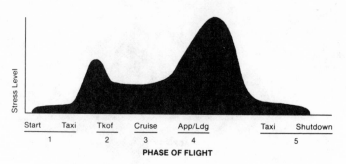

Source: Adapted from Richardson, J. (1978) "CFIT: A Human Factors Problem." *Aerospace Safety, 2,* 3.

2. *High-Task Phase*—Occurs during takeoff and continues throughout the climb. The entire flight crew is usually very busy during this phase.

3. *Passive Activity Phase*—Encompasses the en route portion of the flight. This phase is usually considered routine and boring for most pilots, as it requires little activity beyond monitoring the status of the aircraft and its progress over the ground, and communicating.

As the aircraft progresses toward its destination, stress increases in the cockpit. This occurs due to (a) anticipation of increased workload and (b) accumulation of stress over the course of the flight, hence cumulative effects of stress are experienced.

4. *Preparatory Phase*—Occurs during the approach and landing portions of the flight. During this phase stress is at its highest level for the entire flight. The flight crew is also busiest during this phase. This is the phase during which most pilot-induced accidents occur.

5. *Resolution Phase*—This phase begins right after the aircraft has landed and continues throughout the shutdown of the last engine and the setting of the parking brake.

This profile is highly dynamic. It may change at any time during a flight as environmental conditions change. Preexisting stress will also increase the level of stress experienced by an individual pilot's profile, and may tend to affect other crewmembers, increasing group stress levels in the cockpit.

4

Personality and Psychological Factors

Romance in aviation is not dead. The stereotype of the macho, heroic, battle-loving, barnstorming aviator of yesterday is giving way to a new breed of pilot.

Professional aviation is witnessing a subtle shift from brawn to brains. More pilots are describing themselves as sensitive, concerned, interactive, and aware. This is a far cry from the personality profiles that typify pilots as being defensive, avoidant, isolative, and prone to denial. But why such a dramatic change? During my seven-year investigation, I found that several social forces were coming into play that seem to have accounted for this shift.

The most profound of these social forces is that of society's changing view of sex-role expectations. For the past twenty years men and women have been questioning the rigidly held beliefs about the ways in which men and women are expected to behave.

Men have typically been brought up to be strong, aggressive, intelligent, dominant, territorial, and unemotional. Women's expectations have centered around passiveness, submissiveness, childbearing, childrearing, dependency, and nurturance. A woman's expression of emotions was both expected and tolerated by society. Problems arose when sex-role behaviors were switched by either sex. It was not appropriate for a woman to be too aggressive nor for a man to be too emotional.

Over the years things have been changing. Age-old beliefs of masculine and feminine definitions have been, and continue to be, questioned. Society is seeing that lack of acknowledgment of the different parts of each of our personalities tends to imprison us in ways that lead to inflexibility and consequentially high levels of stress.

Because pilots are social creatures, like the other members of our society, they too have undergone self-evaluation of sex roles.

Another force that has contributed to the shift in behavior observed among pilots is the rapidly changing state of aviation technology. Pilots have had to make major adjustments in their approaches to learning and working in modern aircraft cockpits. Today's pilots are high-tech pilots. Much of their training now focuses on automation and computerization of flight systems and flight-related activities. The current technology of aviation is calling for greater demand on the pilot's intellectual abilities and less demand on his physical capabilities.

Increased knowledge about aviation safety is another reason for the behavioral shift. With the advent of Cockpit Resource Management (CRM) came the widespread realization that the old ways of interacting in the cockpit are obsolete. Pilots are now able to benefit from the wisdom of CRM—wisdom that came only after much unnecessary suffering and sacrifice of human life. With CRM came new ways of behaving—increased assertiveness, consideration of other crewmembers' ideas and opinions, and clearer communication in the cockpit.

Finally, the new breed of pilot is much more psychologically aware. Pilots are realizing that they can no longer deny their marital or relationship problems. They can no longer keep quiet in hopes that things in the work environment will get better. They can no longer hide out in the hope that alcohol or drug problems will go undiscovered.

This shift is a positive one for aviation safety. It marks the beginning of a less stressful professional and personal life-style for the pilot. But change does not happen overnight. It takes time. Even though we are seeing a change in the personality of pilots, we will continue to see the same patterns that we saw in the past. Change cannot come about without awareness. This is why it is important to know which characteristics are commonly seen in pilots' personalities. When we are aware of the personality traits that tend to increase stress, we are more able to do something to change those that exist within ourselves.

PERSONALITY PROFILES

When we talk about a pilot's personality, we are looking at the consistent pattern of attitudes and behaviors that he exhibits. These patterns persist with very little fluctuation from situation to situation.

Over the course of the pilot's lifetime there is some tendency toward modification of personality characteristics, but this is usually not very significant. This modification will come about as a result of life experience, intellectual development, emotional and physical health, and influence from others.

Psychologists who are interested in understanding pilots have, for years, been attracted by the enduring nature of the pilot's personality traits. This has provided a foundation upon which psychologists can predict the behavior of pilots as a group.

Personality profiles are used in aviation for a number of purposes, the most popular of which are employment selection and aviation safety research. My interest here is to present some of the typical personality traits observed among pilots and to see how each of these traits can cause pilot stress. As you review these traits, keep in mind that you may or may not possess all of them. Remember that we are looking at the characteristics observed among a large group of pilots. Also note which of these traits are most like you, somewhat like you, and least like you. These traits are outlined in Table 4–1.

From this list we can infer several attitudes that pilots hold toward pilot stress. First, the high degree of self-sufficiency that many pilots possess tends to provide him with the attitude that he can handle the stressors with which he is faced. While this actually may be so, it is not always the case. This is especially true when the pilot is not aware of the presence of the symptoms of stress he may be experiencing. The pilot's denial of stress and other psychological and physical problems is a difficulty confronting many Aviation Medical Examiners. Self-sufficiency may serve to promote a self-treatment approach taken by the pilot. Self-treatment is effective only when the stress-related problems have not progressed to a serious level and the pilot's self-treatment approach reduces rather than worsens his stress.

Because there is a tendency among some pilots to avoid inner feelings and to attempt to change an undesirable environment, the stressed pilot may become frustrated upon discovering that his immediate environment

Table 4-1
Personality Traits of Pilots

Physically healthy
Lack signs of neurosis
Self-sufficient
Maintain a high need to achieve
Prefer short-range goals to long-range goals
Non-intellectually oriented
Seek responsibility and novelty
Male pilots are unconflicted with other males
Male pilots exhibit anxiety when feeling too close
    to women
Emotionally avoidant
More concerned with modifying their
    environment than changing their own
    behavior
Limited choice in activities
Low tolerance toward personal imperfections
Need excitement
Need individual initiative
Ignore and avoid inner feelings
Inner feelings perceived as external
Avoid introspection (looking within one's own
    mind or feelings)
Cautious about close relationships
Avoid revealing true feelings
Avoid brooding and fighting
Rarely become tearful
Use humor to cope with anxiety or stress
Keep thoughts concrete
Have difficulty with ambiguous situations
Don't handle failure well
Find it difficult to cope when confronted with
    emotional situations

Source. Ursano, R. (1980) "Stress and Adaptation: The Interaction of the Pilot Personality and Disease." *Aviation, Space and Environmental Medicine, 51*(11), 1245–1249.

cannot be modified. This frustration would evolve from the pilot's unreasonable expectations of his ability to change the environment or realization of his own impotence in his environmental-modification abilities. The result is perceived failure and thus more stress.

Overcontrol translates into lack of flexibility. Pilots who have an excessive need to control their environment tend to be limited in the ways in which they attempt to deal with stressors.

Low tolerance toward personal imperfections often leads to excessive and unreasonable self-demands placed on the pilot. Many pilots appear to be extremely critical of others. However, this magnitude of criticalness is exceeded only by the degree that pilots hold toward themselves. When excessive self-demands are placed on the pilot, self-induced stress emerges.

The avoidance of inner feelings may be particularly dangerous to the pilot. This is because feelings often help people to realize when something is wrong. Anxiety is one such feeling. If the pilot denies the emotional experience of anxiety (or any other emotion, for that matter), the underlying (unconscious) emotional discomfort may lead to physical problems in the body such as pain or illness.

The chronic avoidance of exposing one's true feelings to others is characteristic of the emotionally suppressive pilot. By "stuffing" emotions the pilot increases his stress.

Concrete thinking is limited thinking. By perceiving the world in terms of "absolutes," the pilot will be limited in his ability to creatively adapt to and overcome stressors.

Inability to adapt to social situations tends to limit the pilot's ability to benefit from the support of others. Lack of adaptability often creates feelings of isolation.

NORMS

A norm is a standard of conduct that each member of a particular group is expected to uphold. Many of the attitudes that are shared by pilots develop out of the need for pilots to uphold the norms of their professional group. Airline pilots, for instance, have a norm that says it is not all right for any airline pilot to fly his aircraft in an abrupt manner with passengers aboard. This norm is not a spoken rule, but is understood and accepted by all airline pilots.

In the aviation community pilots have norms that tend to produce high levels of stress. Included here are the expectation to exhibit personal discipline, indifference to pain or pleasure, courage, and composure. These norms support the old stereotype of the heroic pilot mentioned at the beginning of this chapter. The problem is that stress does not fit anywhere in this stereotype, therefore it is often denied. This means that pilots must find other ways of coping with stressors.

HOW PILOTS COPE WITH STRESS

How do pilots cope with stressful situations? Primarily through one or more of the following coping mechanisms that appear to be common:

- Denial
- Suppression
- Humor
- Rationalization
- Projection
- Intellectualization

Denial occurs when the pilot refuses to believe that he is involved in a stressful situation. A Falcon 50 copilot reported:

> I knew that we only had one engine operating, but I wasn't scared. I knew that Bill [the captain] had everything under control. We were going to make it back to the airport, I had no doubt.

When the pilot denies his stressful situation, he often ignores important information that could prevent further escalation of the problem. Furthermore, denial doesn't eliminate a stressor; it only serves to prolong it.

Suppression occurs when the pilot actively forces his thoughts out of conscious awareness: "[W]henever I thought of him I quickly put him out of my mind." It takes a lot of effort to suppress your thoughts. The drawback of this approach is that nothing gets resolved. The intrusive thought keeps popping back into consciousness. This is extremely distracting and stressful.

Humor is fun for everybody only when it isn't being used solely to reduce stress. As a defense against a highly stressful situation, it usually doesn't cut it. Who's fooling whom? If a stressor is present you can laugh until you're blue in the face, but it won't go away until you do something to resolve the problem. A 737 captain related:

> My first officer was a barrel of laughs today. He wasn't his usual self. Then we got to the real issue—he had just received notice that his house was in foreclosure.

In rationalization, excuses are used to justify the pilot's actions. A Learjet captain stated:

> . . . I figured it would be OK to take the risk because we didn't have any passengers aboard. Just cargo.

No matter how good the excuse, if you're lying to yourself you will experience the stress that you are trying to avoid.

With projection the pilot attributes his own undesirable thoughts or desires to other people. A corporate pilot told of her experience:

> One of the pilots came in and reported that everybody that he had come in contact with had been in a bad mood. He told us that everybody must have been having a bad day. We later found out that he was the one who was having a bad day!

Projection is a form of denial. By projecting your thoughts or desires onto others, you don't have to own up to them. After all, they belong to everybody else. This creates problems because it may keep you from obtaining any assistance you may need since you are not able to listen to others. It also ruins relationships if it continues for any length of time. The resulting isolation can create more stress.

Intellectualization is for many pilots a way of emotionally detaching themselves from the stressor. When we employ this coping mechanism, we engage in intellectual analysis rather than experience the physical and emotional burden that stress places upon us. A 737 first officer said:

> I don't let stress bother me. Whenever I'm faced with what you term "a stressor," I look at it, analyze it, and move on.

On the surface this approach appears to make sense. After all, it is rational. The problem with intellectualization lies not in the calm manner that the pilot copes with stress, but in his denial of the physical and emotional pressures of stress. By ignoring these effects, the pilot actually prolongs his stress.

Each of the coping mechanisms presented here have one thing in common: denial. When the pilot closes his eyes to stressful situations, the situations do not necessarily go away. Even when they do disappear, the effects of the stressor become internalized by the pilot, both mentally and physically. These lingering effects eventually show up as stress symptoms. When explaining this to pilots I like to use the analogy of a cup being filled with boiling hot water. The cup represents the pilot; the water represents the stressors. As more and more stressors are placed in the cup, the cup's capacity to contain them decreases. In time the cup becomes full. Should an attempt be made to pour more boiling water into the cup, it will overflow, burning everything it touches. The pilot only has a limited capacity to deal with (contain) stress. Should his capacity be exceeded, it will affect other areas of his life. The effects of his stress will overflow into his personal and professional life, his mental and physical state, and his flying. Unhealthy coping mechanisms such as those just described tend to keep the pilot from being aware that his cup is filling. Denial of this prevents him from engaging in effective stress management. Instead of helping him cope with stress, these unhealthy coping mechanisms increase the pilot's vulnerability to stress.

ACCIDENT-PRONE PILOTS

Inadequate stress coping among pilots can lead to accident proneness. In a survey of 737 naval pilots[1] who had been involved in aviation accidents, it was found that those whose accidents were attributed to pilot error possessed one or more of the following traits or situations:

[1]Alkov, R., Gaynor, Jr., & Borowsky, M. (1985) Pilot Error as a Symptom of Inadequate Stress Coping. *Aviation, Space and Environmental Medicine, 51*(9), 244–247.

- Poor leader
- Lacks maturity and stability
- Financial problems
- Recently engaged to be married
- Recent major career decision
- Not professional in flying
- Difficulty in interpersonal relationships
- Trouble with superiors
- Incapable of quickly assessing potential trouble
- Trouble with peers
- Drinks excessively or has recently changed alcohol intake
- Has no sense of own limitations
- Recent change in personality

The factors falling in the category of "personality factors" that contribute to aircraft accidents are: lack of maturity and stability, lack of ability to assess potential trouble quickly, and inability to sense one's own limitations. From this list we can see that there are a number of stress-producing personality traits and situations of which the pilot should be aware.

"TYPE A" PERSONALITY

No examination of personality factors affecting pilots would be complete without a discussion of the Type A personality. We all know pilots who are highly driven, motivated, time pressured, competitive, and ambitious. You may be one yourself. These pilots are said to possess the Type A personality, which produces self-induced stress.

The Type A's counterpart is the pilot who is more calm and less hurried. This individual is usually not as goal oriented as the Type A and is usually more satisfied generally.

Type A behavior is much more stressful than that of Type B, but can be modified. Pilots who are serious about their health should also be aware that those of us who possess the Type A personality are more prone to coronary heart disease.

Despite this awareness, many Type A pilots do not want to change their behavior. Why? Because it is immediately gratifying. They view their behavior as positive and feel comfortable with it. Employers are usually happy with the Type A pilot because he is a hard worker. For the pilot who does not want to give up his Type A pattern, it would be a good idea to modify it so that negative stress-effects will not interfere with productivity. An important goal of stress management is to help the pilot function at optimum levels without being harmed by stressors.

There are psychological factors that also affect pilots. These factors interact closely with the pilot's personality and can be a source of stress.

THE PILOT'S IDENTITY

For most pilots flying and much that is involved in flying is a major part of their identity. Any threat to the pilot's career or aviation-related activities may be perceived by the pilot as a threat to his identity.

I have seen a number of cases where pilots have experienced tremendously high levels of stress because they were grounded. In each case, the pilot had to face the uncomfortable fact that he would be unable to function as a pilot. Whether the pilot was grounded temporarily or permanently, like a bird who had lost its wings, he was faced with an identity crisis. For the grounded pilot the question always arises: Who am I without my ability to fly?

Nonpilots often cannot imagine why pilots are so attached to flying. They cannot understand the almost addictive need many pilots have for flight. I myself had often wondered what it is that so strongly attracts pilots to aviation. After working with many pilots, I have come to realize that pilots' definitions of themselves are greatly influenced by their aviation involvement—"I am an airline pilot," "I fly DC-10s," "I like mountain flying," "When I fly I feel like I'm at home." These are statements pilots often make when they talk about themselves. They are identity statements. They tell us something about who the person is that is making them. If a threat exists to the content of such statements, which is the case when a pilot loses his medical certificate and can no longer fly, the pilot's identity is also threatened. What do you call an airline pilot who can no longer fly? What does a person who felt like he was at home while flying feel like when he is no longer able to fly? I know a pilot who was adamant about giving up his house and his wife before he would give up his airplane.

Flying contributes to the pilot's identity by defining the roles he takes on and providing him with such needs as responsibility, control, acceptance, status, uniqueness, novelty, and challenge. If anybody or anything threatens to take this away from him, he will usually react very strongly, almost as if his survival were at stake. Some of the situations which, because of the potential threat they pose, are highly stressful to the pilot include:

- Medical examinations
- Check rides
- Illness, disease, or injury
- Furloughs
- Cut in pay
- Conflict with supervisors or peers

When the pilot experiences any of these, whether he is aware of it or not, he should be aware that his potential for stress is high, and that he must take positive steps to reduce his stress.

MENTAL STATE

The mental state of the pilot is reflected by his state of mind. When it is positive, and he is not bogged down by distracting thoughts or emotional troubles, the pilot is more able to function in the cockpit. But when the pilot is stressed, it is difficult for him to maintain a positive attitude. He may find himself working very hard just to meet minimally acceptable levels of performance. This is a situation that the pilot will want to avoid.

One's mental state is influenced by a number of factors, including illness, fear, and anxiety. When the pilot experiences mental or physical illness, his stress increases. This results in limited capacity to cope with further stressors. The pilot is forced to put his energies into dealing with the illness if he wishes to overcome it.

Fortunately, most pilots do not suffer from serious mental illness. Many are screened out of professional aviation through employment and psychological interviewing and testing. Those who are missed in the screening process usually wind up leaving aviation, due to a lack of coping skills necessary to meet the daily challenges found in most aviation jobs. For the majority of pilots it is stressors, rather than mental illness, that causes them to possess a negative mental state.

Physical illness can also contribute to a negative mental state. When the pilot is not feeling well physically, he may find it very difficult to approach his flight duties with enthusiasm. Physical illness often leads to stress, which leaves the pilot with less available coping energy.

One of the most stressful things a pilot can experience is fear and the anxiety it produces. Fear and anxiety can keep a pilot from feeling comfortable when he is placed in certain situations. Many things can trigger fear and anxiety in pilots and it is important for the pilot to find out what they are so he can take steps to overcome them.

Many pilots are not aware of the fact that all pilots have fears associated with flying. These fears can be associated with certain phases of flight. For example, one aviator expressed his fears:

> I find myself most fearful during the initial climbout. We're moving fast while the small guys out there in those Cessnas and Pipers are crawling. My biggest fear is that we won't see one of them and we'll have a midair.

Similarly, the fear might be associated with operations in certain types of meteorologic conditions:

> I hate turbulence. Every time I encounter it I feel my anxiety increasing. . . . I just don't like it one bit.

Other fears that pilots have reported to me include:

- Flying alone
- Flying into busy airports
- Emergencies
- Structural fire in flight
- Operating certain types of aircraft
- Flying at night
- Check rides
- Midair collisions
- Flying over the ocean
- Landing at the wrong airport
- Making a fool of oneself in front of peers
- Losing medical certificate

- Unintentionally violating FARs
- Being permanently grounded
- Structural or mechanical failures in flight
- Terrorism
- Misunderstanding and not complying with ATC instructions
- Crashing the aircraft

Many of the fears pilots have are about real things that can happen. Caution and awareness at all times while operating any aircraft is a must. It is when fear and anxiety are exaggerated and cause much discomfort for the pilot that a problem does exist. The problem must be dealt with because the anxiety accompanying fear tends to cause stress, which interferes with the pilot's performance. Some of the indicators I use to help pilots decide when they should seek professional assistance from a psychotherapist to deal with their fears are: obsessive thoughts about the feared object or situation; inability to sleep; increased smoking or drinking; rapid gain or loss of weight; overreaction or panic when placed in the feared situation; or a tendency to want to avoid flying because of the fear. If one or more of these symptoms is experienced by the pilot, he should seek professional help.

It is important for pilots to know that something can be done about the fear and anxiety they experience. For most pilots who acknowledge their fears, there is some degree of embarrassment. What I am finding, though, is that pilots are starting to own up to their fears and are seeking help. Many of the pilots with whom I have worked have been able to work through their fears and were able to continue flying. These pilots were not labeled as mentally ill—they were healthy individuals who were responsible enough to eliminate a major source of stress in their lives.

5

Physiological Factors

The threat of having an Aviation Medical Examiner discover that a problem exists that will cause the pilot to be declared unfit for flight becomes more real for the pilot as he grows older. Unmanaged stress dramatically increases the chances of this happening at a much earlier age. With the growing number of stressors in professional aviation, pilots are being forced to become increasingly more aware of the importance of health maintenance and preventive medicine. They are realizing that it is never too early, nor is it too late, to start taking care of themselves.

This chapter will examine the areas where pilots tend to be physiologically vulnerable to stress. Awareness of these areas can prepare the pilot to take preventive measures to protect himself from such problems.

CARDIOVASCULAR DISEASE

Cardiovascular disease is the leading cause of death, sudden incapacitation, and disability among pilots. It also accounts for more than 50% of all cases of early retirement among airline pilots. Not surprisingly, it is the leading cause of death in highly developed nations and the high-tech world of professional aviation.

What is cardiovascular disease? It is any form of disease that affects the heart and vascular systems. Under normal conditions the heart, which is a muscle that contains four chambers through which blood circulates, contracts, and relaxes. During the contraction phase, pressure within these chambers increases, forcing the blood out of the heart through many miles of arteries into the body. This contraction phase is followed by relaxation of the heart muscle, at which time the chambers of the heart fill with blood. This entire process is repeated an average of sixty to eighty times per minute in the average adult. For life to be sustained, this process must continue so that the body will receive oxygen and minerals, the vital nutritional constituents of the blood.

When pilots are faced with stress, this process speeds up. The heart pumps faster and works harder to provide the body with increased blood flow so that it can meet the demands of any emergency situation that it faces. When stress becomes chronic, the heart is forced to work too hard. Chronic stress frequently leads to other conditions such as hypertension, atherosclerosis, and arrhythmias. When there is a lack of oxygenation to the heart muscle, pilots experience a "heart attack."

HYPERTENSION

The pressure of the blood against the arterial walls at any given time is known as "blood pressure." There are two readings that the Aviation Medical Examiner evaluates. The first is the systolic measure, which represents the pressure of the blood against the artery walls during the contraction phase of heart pumping. The second reading is the diastolic measure, or the measure which represents the arterial pressure during the relaxation phase. These readings are taken with the use of the blood pressure cuff, or the sphygmomanometer. The normal systolic range is about 100 to 140 millimeters of mercury (mmHg), while the normal diastolic range is about 60 to 90 mmHg. Blood pressure is reported as the systolic over the diastolic reading, for example, 120/80 mmHg.

When the pilot is under stress specific hormones are activated and blood pressure increases. This causes the arterial walls to provide increased resistance so that the body will be assured of the necessary blood supply that it may need to meet the stressor's demands. Should the body be under constant stress, it will not receive feedback via the nervous system to allow it to return to a less anxious state. The result is hypertension (chronic high blood pressure). This condition is characterized by blood pressure readings which exceed 160/95 mmHg. If this condition remains chronic the pilot will be under increased risk of heart attack because the heart will be forced to work harder. Also, chronic hypertension causes an increased weakness of the vessel walls, predisposing the pilot to a cerebral vascular accident—or stroke. This is the rupturing of a blood vessel in the brain. It can lead to paralysis or even death.

The biggest danger of hypertension lies in its lack of symptoms. Hypertension often goes unnoticed until it is either discovered by the Aviation Medical Examiner during the pilot's flight physical, or when the pilot experiences sudden serious problems. This is why the pilot must have his blood pressure checked regularly.

At present, the aim of treatment for hypertension focuses on lowering the pilot's blood pressure. This can be accomplished through change in diet (for example, reduction in salt intake), elimination of cigarette smoking, weight loss (if the pilot is overweight or obese), and stress management. In some cases, the Aviation Medical Examiner may choose to prescribe antihypertensive medication.

ATHEROSCLEROSIS

Atherosclerosis is another vascular problem that can lead to cardiovascular disease. It is a condition in which fatty substances containing cholesterol collect on the arterial walls. This leads to hardening of the arteries. As the arteries harden and the occlusion of the arteries takes place due to fatty substance buildup, bloodflow becomes greatly restricted. This, too, forces the heart to work harder. In addition to a heart attack, another risk can present itself. That is the risk of bulging in the wall of an artery. This bulge, or "aneurism," may balloon out until it bursts. There is a third risk factor that can occur with atherosclerosis, which is the increased risk of blood clotting which can take place in the occluded artery. Should clotting occur, it is possible for a piece of the clot to break free, eventually lodging itself in another part of the body. The blood clot can lead to a stroke, can cause an aneurism, or may cause both.

Atherosclerosis is best treated through preventive means. A high-cholesterol diet should be replaced with a low-cholesterol diet. Whether or not a pilot is overweight, there may nonetheless be high serum levels of cholesterol in the blood which must be reduced. A blood test helps physicians determine whether serum levels are high. Daily physical exercise is also helpful because it causes the blood to circulate more efficiently throughout the body. Other forms of treatment include medication and, in serious cases, surgical intervention.

ARRHYTHMIAS

An arrhythmia is an abnormal heartbeat. This is caused by damage to the heart itself, which might result from lack of adequate blood supply, and thus oxygen, to sustain the heart muscle; or it can be caused by other means such as drug or alcohol use; or may be the result of a congenital condition.

Arrhythmias range from mild, as in the case of an occasional skipped beat, to very serious, as occurs during fibrillation, where the heart is beating so rapidly and wildly that it cannot adequately pump blood to the body.

Once again, a preventive approach is important. Arrhythmias that are detected early can be treated through proper diet and exercise. Obesity, smoking, and stress are contributors. Medication can also be prescribed to treat arrhythmias. Serious cases may require implantation of a heart pacemaker, a device that helps normalize the heartbeat.

DRUG USE

Moral and ethical implications of illicit drug use are outside the purview of this book, but it is helpful to know about the relationship between drug use and stress, as well as to know how to obtain help to deal with this problem. When a person is unable to stop using any drug, *right now*—that is, cold turkey—assistance is needed. All pilots must make the choice: fly or use drugs. These are the only choices, because if a pilot is using drugs and continues to fly, he is not only a danger to himself, but is also a danger to others. This is an extremely serious problem.

Aside from the fact that drug use impairs mental and physical functioning, and that it is a major threat to aviation safety, there is another important reason why not to use them: they are incredibly stress-producing. Most pilots who use drugs use them as a stress-management tool. But, like a fox in sheep's clothing, drugs have a way of creating stress that goes unobserved by the user. Everyone around the user is aware of the negative effects—everyone, that is, but the user—at least, not until these negative effects cause serious problems. The problems include chronic fatigue, difficulty in interpersonal relationships, increased risk-taking in the cockpit, increased absenteeism, emotional displays, extreme weight gain or loss, marital problems. If the drug use goes unnoticed by others, the pilot may be lulled into a false sense of security. He may believe that he is "handling the drug well." Pilots who are covert drug users tend to avoid asking themselves when their luck might take a turn for the worse—will the effects finally catch up with him while he is flying? If so, when? While shooting an ILS approach to minimums? Or maybe it might occur while shooting a category-two approach.

There is plenty of help available for pilots who use drugs. If you are afraid of losing your medical certificate, you may first want to inquire anonymously or state that you are inquiring for a friend, or that you are just wondering how such a problem would be handled. My personal position is that I would rather see a pilot get help anonymously than to see him avoid obtaining assistance for fear of being permanently grounded. A number of airlines have employee-assistance programs (EAPs) that are willing to work with pilots to help them overcome their drug problems. In some cases the pilot's flying privileges are not even suspended. If such a program is not available to you, you might seek help through one of many reputable drug programs such as Narcotics Anonymous (NA), Cocaine Anonymous (CA), and in- and outpatient treatment programs. Do not hesitate to seek help if you need it. You won't be the first pilot to do so, nor will you be the last. Everybody who uses drugs runs the risk of having to seek professional assistance to discontinue their use: for instance, 85% of all cocaine users are unable to discontinue its use without some form of outside intervention.

ALCOHOL

The FAA has indicated that alcohol education has lowered the rate of alcohol-related aircraft accidents. However, despite the FAA's educational efforts, alcohol abuse continues to be a serious problem in professional aviation. If the incidence of alcohol abuse for the aviation community is equivalent to that of society as a whole, it is estimated that 7% of all pilots have a drinking problem. Unlike the use of other drugs, alcohol use is not chastised by the aviation community—that is, so long as its use does not take place outside the legal time limits prior to flight.

Why do pilots drink? For several reasons, which include social purposes, to increase confidence, and to develop a sense of personal power. Many pilots drink to relax. Here again, the pilot must become aware of the fact that alcohol is, as with any other chemical substance, a poor stress-management tool. As the pilot feels more and more euphoric, stress tends to build unconsciously.

How can you tell if you have a drinking problem? Two

methods have been helpful: (1) Abstain from all drinking for a period of one month. If you find it difficult to avoid drinking, or if you experience withdrawal symptoms (edginess, irritability, jumpiness), a problem exists; (2) A self-assessment of your life can provide good insight. If you look at your life and find that it has reached the point where it is no longer manageable, you need help. Also be alert for other signs of an alcohol problem such as the presence of an "enabler" in your life. Family members or friends often take on the enabler role by enabling or supporting the pilot's drinking problem. Enablers work in different ways. They may cover up for the alcoholic (wife calls the pilot's employer and says her husband is ill, while in fact he is intoxicated or hung over), or they may encourage the alcohol use ("You've been under a lot of stress—why don't you have a drink?"). The enabler may even have an alcohol problem himself and help the pilot maintain the habit in order to have someone to drink with ("Boy, that was a tough flight—let's go have a couple of beers"). Enablers often work hard to keep the pilot from overcoming his problem, even though they may strongly claim to want the pilot to stop drinking. Why? Because change is threatening. If the pilot stops drinking, it often forces the enabler to have to relate to the pilot differently. This is a difficult task for many people. Drug users should also beware of the enabler.

Treatment of an alcohol problem is widely available. All a person must do is ask for it. The company's EAP is an excellent place to start. Many airlines offer help to pilots who have an alcohol problem, and in many cases, the pilot is permitted to continue flying while receiving treatment.

Alcoholics Anonymous (AA) continues to have the number-one treatment-success rate. Meetings are easily accessed and are only a telephone call away. For the alcoholic's family, there is Alanon and Alateen (for teenage children). Both of these groups help their members live healthier life-styles.

MEDICATION

Certain prescription and over-the-counter medications can affect the pilot's normal mental and physical functioning. Side effects as well as indicated effects may also limit the pilot's ability to withstand and cope with stress.

Several medication side effects may contribute to pilot error and lead to aircraft accidents. These are: drowsiness associated with antihistamine use, decreased alertness with tranquilizer use, lack of judgment and feelings of false confidence with the use of reducing agents and "pep" pills, and suppression of mental alertness with the use of barbiturates, nerve tonics, and painkillers. Other dangers that may accompany medication use include drug allergies, change of medication effects due to high altitude or "G" forces, and drug combination effects.

The injury, illness, or disease that is responsible for necessitating the use of medication by the pilot is a good indicator of stress, which the pilot should examine. If the condition for which the pilot must take medication is one that will cause further stress if he flies, he should seriously consider waiting until the condition improves. This should be done regardless of the fact that the medications being used will not interfere with the pilot's operation of the aircraft.

I had a very painful skin rash. The Aviation Medical Examiner who examined it said that it would go away within a few days. He gave me some ointment to put on it. Even though he told me that I would be able to fly with the rash and with the medication, I chose not to because I knew that my mind would be on the pain and not on my flying.

The stress and side effects of any medication used should be checked out with the AME prior to flight. These physicians are specially trained to provide information that will help the pilot choose whether to go or not go.

FATIGUE

Fatigue has been defined by the FAA as "a depletion of body energy reserves, leading to below-par performance." Two types of fatigue have been characterized: chronic and acute.

Chronic (long-term) fatigue may be of emotional or physical origin. Professional assistance is recommended with this form of fatigue.

Acute fatigue may come about from several causes, which include mild hypoxia, emotional stress, physical stress, depletion of physical energy, lack of sleep, poor nutrition, poor physical health, and excitement. Adequate amounts of rest, exercise, a proper diet, and effective stress-management are all helpful for overcoming and preventing fatigue.

Insomnia (the inability to sleep) is not an unusual complaint of pilots and may contribute to fatigue. Pilots who suffer from insomnia may find it difficult to fall asleep, they may experience difficulty remaining asleep, or they may be afflicted by both of these problems. Some of the causes of insomnia include obsessive thoughts about unresolved issues in the pilot's personal or professional life; excessive intake of coffee, tea, or other caffeinated beverages; anxiety; depression; worry; lack of adjustment to an unfamiliar environment; or discomfort caused by heat, cold, humidity, pain, etc.

Some pilots dream about not being asleep, only to awaken after a number of hours, feeling fatigued. This is a frustrating situation that fortunately most of them don't experience.

There are steps pilots can take to relieve insomnia. Relaxation exercises (see Chapter 10) are often helpful in releasing tension and anxiety. They should be used prior to sleep. Avoidance of meals or snacks just prior to sleep can also be helpful. Pilots with insomnia should think twice before drinking caffeinated beverages. Also, a number of pilots have informed me of their success with warm baths just prior to sleep. In addition to the effects of muscle relaxation and soothing, the act of warming the body appears to have a beneficial effect on sleep. Warm milk also seems to do the trick. There is a sound scientific reason for this: warm milk contains L-Tryptophane, an amino acid that aids in sleep. L-Tryptophane is also available in tablet form and can be purchased as a dietary supplement in most health food stores. Though L-Tryptophane is a natural substance and is not considered a drug, anyone thinking about using it should first consult their AME to see how it can best be incorporated into the diet.

Another issue to be addressed is that of sleeping medications. The word is out in the medical community that they can cause insomnia. If not properly prescribed, sleeping medications can cause abnormal sleep. When they are taken, dream sleep is suppressed. When the medication is withdrawn, dreams may reappear much more vividly. This may lead to sleeplessness and nightmares. Hence, the vicious circle begins: the frightened individual demands more pills to avoid his own overzealous dreaming activity.

JET LAG

The relationship between time and stress is well understood by the pilot when we speak of "delays," "schedules," and "appointments." But when the term "jet lag" is mentioned, the pilot's understanding of the time-stress relationship moves from clarity to vagueness.

We have all experienced some symptoms of jet lag after a long flight—disorientation, confusion, a general feeling of discomfort and uneasiness, distortions of time and distance, sleep disturbances, short-term memory loss, irritability, time-inappropriate occurrence of hunger and elimination, and digestive problems. We are also well aware of the fatigue that accompanies jet lag (which, incidentally, is the most dangerous symptom to the pilot). Many pilots, however, do not really know what jet lag really is.

. . . I know it has something to do with crossing time zones.

. . . I'm aware of the fact that I feel awful for days after I take the run to the east coast. But what is jet lag? I'm not quite sure.

These are typical responses to this commonly experienced phenomenon in aviation. They are responses that render the pilot defenseless to jet lag, for without knowledge of its basic cause, the pilot is unable to take steps to minimize its effects.

The first step toward gaining more insight into the

cause of jet lag is the demystification of the phenomenon. The label "jet lag" is a good place to start. Contrary to popular belief, you do not have to fly in jet aircraft to experience the symptoms of jet lag. The term "jet lag" is somewhat misleading because its effects are not really dependent upon flying in jet aircraft. Symptoms can be experienced regardless of the mode of transportation used. Jet aircraft are singled out because they represent the fastest mode of transportation available (with the exception of rocket-powered aircraft, which are not practical for commercial use). Modes of transportation that travel farther in a shorter time tend to help us experience jet-lag symptoms in a much more pronounced manner.

To demystify this phenomenon further, it is helpful to look at one of the most basic concepts found in nature—the concept of "rhythm." Everything around us is influenced by rhythm. The ocean tides ebb and flow with rhythm; morning and evening temperature changes, which take place over the land and sea, occur with rhythm; the sun rises and descends in accordance with rhythm. Each of these environmental occurrences takes place regularly over a cycle of twenty-four hours. These twenty-four-hour rhythm cycles are known as "circadian rhythms."

Just as rhythm exists in the environment, it also governs the physiological processes that occur within our bodies. The heart beats with a rhythm of its own; our sleep and breathing patterns are rhythmic; our internal temperature undergoes predictable variations, reaching its highest level during periods when we are most active. All of these activities seem to be influenced by many internal body clocks that tell the body what should take place and when. Many of these internal clocks are also paired with the circadian rhythm cycle. During the twenty-four-hour day, we eat, sleep, and eliminate waste at specific times.

Jet-lag symptoms occur after crossing time zones. Why is this so? Because humans respond internally to environmental cues such as sunrise and sunset—cues that occur during the circadian (twenty-four-hour) period. These external cues help the pilot's internal body clocks know when he should eat, sleep, eliminate, become more active, socialize, etc. When time zones are crossed, the environmental cues change. The sun no longer rises or sets at the same time of day or night. The daily temperature is no longer the same. In some parts of the world the days may be longer, while the nights are shorter. The temperature may change very little or the change may be dramatic. All of these environmental changes send the many internal body clocks into a state of confusion. In addition, the various systems of the body lose their synchronicity with each other.

Resynchronization of the body's biological clocks takes time because these clocks must readjust to the external cues in the new environment.

The effects of jet lag tend to persist in some pilots for a few days after reaching their destination, while for other pilots, jet-lag symptoms may last for a period of one week or longer. For most pilots, the symptoms last longer following flights in an easterly direction, as opposed to westbound flights.

Jet lag can be a chronic problem for pilots, especially for those who fly in nonscheduled service operations, military operations, and transcontinental scheduled service.

How can the effects of jet lag be minimized? There are several steps that the pilot can take. The first involves preflight preparation. The pilot should restrict drinking of caffeinated beverages to the morning hours for westbound flights and to the evening hours for eastbound flights. Preflight action should also include the consumption of foods rich in B complex, and vitamins E and C. These vitamin-rich foods should also be consumed after arriving at the destination.

During the flight, the pilot should drink at least two glasses of water per hour. This will help him to avoid the dehydration typically experienced in flight due to high cabin altitudes. Dehydration can contribute to jet lag.

After arrival, the pilot should avoid consumption of caffeinated beverages altogether in the morning. He should also eat a high-protein meal at breakfast and lunchtime. A high-carbohydrate meal should be eaten in the evening.

The pilot should go to bed earlier than usual if he has traveled eastbound, and he should go to bed at his usual time (use the destination clock to determine this) when his travel has taken him westbound.

Some pilots are tempted to use alcohol or sleeping pills to help them sleep. These should be avoided, as they tend to worsen the effects of jet lag. Instead, the pilot will find it more beneficial to promote sleep using the relaxation techniques presented in Chapter 10.

6

Environmental, Experiential, and Sociocultural Factors

ENVIRONMENTAL FACTORS

The environment in which the pilot lives and works can contribute to stress. Environmental factors include the pilot's work climate (both outside and inside the cockpit); his physical environment both outside and inside the aircraft, while operating the aircraft on the ground and in flight; and his personal (domestic or social) environmental conditions.

Work Climate—Outside the Cockpit

There are times when every pilot finds his work environment a major source of stress. When this occurs, the pilot's own stress can cause stress in others.

One form of stress that occurs within the work environment comes from the intrinsically stressful nature of the pilot's job. Job underload and overload are two examples of job-related intrinsic stress. During periods of job underload, the pilot finds that there is not enough for him to do. Passively waiting for something to do is stressful for most pilots. A nonscheduled charter pilot shared his experience of job underload with me:

> You know, I love to fly. If it weren't for flying I would never be sitting here [in a pilots' lounge at Palm Springs Airport] in the middle of the night with nothing to do. I think the toughest part of this job is just sitting around and waiting. That's how aviation is—you hurry to get to your destination so that you can wait.

Job overload, or having too much work to do, is another source of stress. When the job is designed to keep the pilot working all of the time, it can lead to heavy pressure on him.

> Commuter flying is extremely demanding. We're expected to fly safely for ten hours a day. We take off and land at many different airports every day. We operate at lower altitudes, which means that we must contend with all kinds of traffic and all kinds of pilots. On top of it all, the paperwork is phenomenal. It gets tough at times.

Danger poses another source of job-related stress. Aviation is not without its threat of danger to the pilot. Some types of operations are obviously more dangerous than others, but danger nonetheless exists at all times while operating aircraft. An air-evacuation pilot related:

> Chopper flying is a thrill to most of us, but there are times when things can and do get pretty hairy. There's always a risk of danger.

When the pilot experiences too much stress on the job, the fun and enjoyment can disappear very quickly. Anxiety, depression, and physical problems can contribute to lack of job satisfaction.

When I first started flying for this company I couldn't wait to get to work. But after a while, the long hours and pressure started getting to me. I feel physically run down and emotionally drained.

The pilot's role in the company he works for can be another source of work-related stress. When role ambiguity (conflicting demands on the job) occurs, the pilot may find it difficult to fully function in his role as pilot. An air charter captain described his experience with role ambiguity:

We were on the ramp at Reno airport. There were five airplanes in our charter group. When the passengers arrived it was discovered that five airplanes wouldn't be enough. I called the dispatcher in L.A. He told me that I should take care of the situation, and that he couldn't because he was busy. I wound up having to do his job and my own. It was extremely stressful. Besides myself, the passengers and the crewmembers were all anxious. When I finally coordinated things, I got in my airplane and became even more stressed at the thought of having to fly to San Francisco in the bad weather that I knew I was going to encounter along my route.

The situation that this pilot experienced was one that set the stage for another source of stress. This is role conflict. Anytime one person on the job must take on the duties of another—duties that are not prescribed in the person's original job role—conflict can occur. The conflict one experiences in this case is over two dissimilar roles (for example, pilot and dispatcher). Pilot duties (or roles) include preflight action and safe operation of the aircraft. They do not include chartering other aircraft, bargaining for the lowest cost, coordinating flight crews and handling catering arrangements for a number of aircraft. Conflict occurs when other nonpilot duties call for full attention that should be accorded to pilot duties. In role conflict, the pilot is forced to subordinate some aspects of each role to accomplish more than he should have to handle. By wearing two or more hats, energy is taken away from the pilot's most important role: that of total attention to the safe and efficient conduct of his flight.

Another job-related stressor intrinsic to aviation is the pilot's responsibility for the safety of others. This is, as every pilot will admit, a concern that is ever present in his thinking. It also puts pressure on him to perform safely:

> I know that it's up to me and my crew to get the 200 passengers to their destination safely. Sometimes it creates a lot of stress for me to worry about the safety of my passengers. This is particularly true when I'm flying in meteorological conditions where all I really want to think about is the airplane.

Stress in the work environment can also be influenced by the types of relationships the pilot has with others. Pilots who have poor relationships with others, and who lack social support, generally experience higher levels of stress.

Other sources of occupational stress outside the cockpit include overpromotion (the pilot who is promoted before he is emotionally ready and/or experienced enough to handle the new job), underpromotion (the pilot who is held back from promotion), and lack of job security (which affects most pilots). For female pilots, lack of promotion because of discriminatory practices can account for major stress. For both male and female pilots, office politics also continue to create much stress.

The effects of occupational stress are not limited to the work environment. When work-related stressors are brought home, or when domestic problems are brought into the work environment, increased stress and conflict may be experienced. Dual-career marriages (where both partners have careers) are a major source of stress for some pilots. When the husband and wife are both employed (especially in different professions), problems may develop. One problem which may affect the pilot is the conflict between the company's demand for mobility (for example, relocation) and the spouse's inability to be mobile owing to his or her own career needs and demands.

Work Climate—Inside the Cockpit

The work climate inside the cockpit is influenced by the same factors that cause stress in the pilot's work environment outside the cockpit. The job-related intrinsic stressors relevant to the cockpit environment include length of duty time, time of day or night that the flight is being conducted, job underload and overload, and the highly stressful flight segments as presented on the Pilot Stress profile (Figure 3-4).

In the cockpit, the pilot's role in his company can be a major source of stress. His role as captain, first officer, or second officer is characterized by the expected responsibilities and duties that are demanded of him in the cockpit. For instance, the airline captain and the military aircraft commander have the similar role of functioning as the final authority as to the operation of the aircraft.

In some cases role ambiguity and role conflicts between crewmembers may occur. When this happens crew coordination can break down. The redundancy that has been introduced into multicrew aircraft operations for the purpose of aviation safety tends to be reduced when role ambiguity and role conflicts occur.

> The captain busted his assigned altitude twice. When I called him on it he told me to keep quiet. He told me that he knew what he was doing. I wouldn't have any part of that. It was obvious that he didn't know what he was doing.

In the above scenario the captain overplayed his role as the authority figure in the cockpit. When the first officer called him on his errors, he became defensive. This set the stage for role conflict in the cockpit. The first officer had to assert himself and take the command position so that the captain could be made aware of his potentially dangerous actions. Neither pilot was comfortable with the effects of role reversal. The first officer did, however, assert himself until the captain acknowledged his need to correct his actions.

Poor crew coordination can be very stressful for each pilot involved. In several accidents involving controlled flight into terrain (CFIT), where no apparent mechanical failures could be attributed to the cause of the accident, human error was found to be the cause. Factors that contribute to poor crew coordination include the manner in which command is accepted and exercised, lack of coordination of the flight crew, perceptions of each crewmember's responsibilities, and lack of mutual respect.

When good crew coordination exists, role ambiguity and role conflict decrease. The result is a less stressful and much safer cockpit work environment.

The pilot's career development may also be a stressful

factor in the cockpit. The pilot who has not been promoted may resent his current duties, while the pilot who has been promoted prematurely may harbor fear and doubt concerning his abilities, duties, and responsibilities. The overpromoted pilot may, in fact, lack the necessary technical and interpersonal skills for the new position. Either of these situations may lead to job dissatisfaction which can further lead to stress. Pilots with greater ability to perform their duties are less vulnerable to stress on the job.

As I indicated earlier, stressors from the pilot's personal life may be brought into the work environment. The same is true for the cockpit work environment. Some of these stressors include dual-career marriages, divorce, death of a family member, and spousal disagreements and arguments.

Physical Environment—Outside the Cockpit

A number of physical environmental factors outside the cockpit may increase pilot stress levels. These include adverse meteorological conditions, overcongested airspace, night operations, excessive glare from the sun, high-altitude flight, flight over water or mountainous terrain, and flight in unfamiliar surroundings. The effects of these stressors may be increased workload, boredom, fear and anxiety, increased physiological demands (such as the frequent need to urinate or the need for more oxygen), and worry. A 747 first officer talks about his concerns regarding extended overwater flight:

> I get anxious about crossing the Atlantic Ocean. I know we have four engines, but the thought of being over a large body of water with no land within hundreds of miles is one that can cause me to experience stress.

Physical Environment—Inside the Cockpit

The cockpit's internal physical environment may also produce stress on the pilot.

Noise is a common stressor for pilots who fly rotary, propeller-driven, turbopropeller-driven, and some jet-powered aircraft. It can cause irritability and nervousness, two factors that can interfere with the pilot's ability to think and concentrate. Decreased hearing is an obvious effect of noise, but stress might be much less apparent. This is why pilots must take precautions to protect themselves.

After testing a number of earplugs and headsets, I found that the simple sponge-rubber foam earplugs seem to work best for me. They don't weigh much, they expand and contract with pressure changes that naturally occur in flight, and they aren't uncomfortable. Other pilots may find different types of ear-protection devices work better or are more comfortable. Whatever choice he makes, he should be sure that his hearing is protected when flying in noisy cockpit environments. Exposure to decibel levels above 80 will lead to some hearing loss, while decibel levels between 100 and 125 for short periods can cause temporary deafness. Permanent deafness can result from exposure to noise above 150 decibels.

Another factor that might lead to stress in the cockpit work environment is thermal stress. This is caused by excessive and prolonged exposure to heat, and may come about through continued flight in very hot external environments (such as desert climates) with a faulty on-board environmental system. Thermal stress can cause heat exhaustion (due to water or salt depletion in the body), heatstroke (due to failure of the body to regulate its temperature properly), or heat cramps (caused by excessive loss of salt from the body).

Other physical factors that may cause stress in the cockpit include very cold cockpit environments, a brightly lit cockpit, cigarette (or pipe or cigar) smoking in the cockpit (inhaled cigarette, pipe, or cigar smoke robs the body of oxygen), unusual flight attitudes, and faulty pressurization leading to inner-ear discomfort and possibly hypoxia.

Pilots must keep in mind that if the cockpit is not a comfortable work environment, stress will inevitably occur.

Personal Environment

The pilot's personal environment represents the conditions under which he operates in his personal life. Should his personal environment contain problematic situations, stress will be experienced.

The pilot's social conditions are also part of his personal environment. These include friendships, educational strivings, involvement in hobbies, entertainment, rest and relaxation practices, and aesthetic pursuits (such as art and music appreciation).

EXPERIENTIAL FACTORS

The inner subjective experiences of the pilot tend to affect his mode of dealing with the routine and not-so-routine stressors that are part of his profession.

I had to depend solely on pilots' reports about their experiences to understand how experiential factors contribute to pilot stress. There are two possible explanations for the lack of formal scientific research in this area. First, it is difficult to conduct research on one's subjective experiences. Secondly, it is difficult for pilots to communicate their subjective experiences. In the process of disclosing one's personal experiences, much is lost. The best that can be hoped for are accurate descriptions, which always fall short of exact experiences. I can personally recall an experience that I had while flying IFR at night, while alone at the controls. I was flying southbound from the Los Angeles area to San Diego. The coastal area was covered with low-level stratus clouds. After departing the airport, I climbed and leveled off at 5,000 feet. To my amazement, the tops were exactly at my cruising altitude. The moon was brightly lit and cast the most beautiful illumination of the cloud tops that I had ever seen. As if that weren't enough, the airplane's wings sat perched on top of the sheetlike clouds. As I flew down the coast it felt like I was floating rather than flying. The slightly uneven cloud tops formed a cushion upon which my wings seemed to glide. It felt like I was at the controls of a hydrofoil rather than an airplane. The experience was a fantastic one and one that I'm sure could be experienced only once in a lifetime. At the time, I felt like I had died and gone to heaven. The sad thing is that unless you have experienced something like this for yourself, my description of this event can never come close to expressing the euphoric experience I had that night over Los Angeles. This is the dilemma all pilots face in some form or another. The pilot's words don't always help others fully understand his experience. Not feeling understood can, at times, be stressful.

There are many areas in which the pilot has experiences that are unique to those who fly, and these are areas of potential stress.

Training

The pilot's training is often a highly stressful experience. Much material is learned during many hours each day for periods lasting from five days to one month or longer.

As information regarding aircraft systems; normal, irregular, and emergency procedures; and crew coordination are repetitively experienced, the pilot often tends to think about this material obsessively, even when out of the training environment. Most pilots report that they often dream about the training material. A DC-10 first officer who was in the process of upgrading to the left seat related his dreams:

> You know, ever since I started my upgrade training, I haven't gotten a good night's sleep. I keep dreaming that I'm still at the flight academy. Last night I must have shot 100 ILS approaches. Every time I completed one, I could hear the instructor say, "Okay, Frank, let's do one more."

Training-related stress can cause the pilot's self-doubts to surface, increasing the intensity of the training situation. The more intensive the training, the greater the potential for stress. It appears that the pilot who has previous knowledge in the area of training that he is receiving will generally experience less stress. A 737 first officer who had just been hired by a major airline addressed the issue:

> I'm glad I had prior formal jet training. I skated through the airline's pilot training program. I sure felt sorry for the pilots who hadn't flown jets. A lot of them really had a time of it. Some of them were even dropped from the program.

Examinations

Though they are a routine part of professional aviation, examinations cause heavy stress for many pilots. These examinations include medical exams, sim checks, flight check rides, route checks, and written and oral examinations. Competency does not always remove the anxiety from the examination process. Many competent pilots have reported that expectation of a difficult examination, fear of forgetting information or procedures, fear of losing flight privileges, fear of loss of license or medical certificate, fear of criticism from peers for making errors, fear of failing, fear of loss of job and life-style, and performance anxiety account for much of the stress associated with examinations in professional aviation.

Perceptions

For the most part, a pilot perceives the world like most other people. The difference, however, is in his aviation-related perceptions.

Pilot training has an effect on one's perceptions. When the pilot enters training, he perceives flight differently from the experienced pilot. With time, knowledge, and development of skills, the pilot's perceptions change. This accounts for the lack of understanding that those who do not fly exhibit when the pilot attempts to describe his experiences as a pilot. The feelings of not being understood and, in many cases, the actual reality of it, can lead to stress and also to tense domestic situations.

Common Language

Group norms dictate common language. Several purposes exist for this phenomenon, including the development and utilization of terms to describe common experiences, the use of terminology to publicly communicate confidential information, acknowledgment of group identity, and the use of terminology to discuss an area of specialized knowledge.

Comaraderie within the group is strengthened by common language, but pilots often experience isolation and alienation from those outside the group. This may include isolation and alienation from family members, as the language that is common to the professional pilot may not be understood by the family. As one pilot described the problem:

> My husband has always been very supportive of my profession as an airline pilot. I often take it for granted that he lacks knowledge of sophisticated aircraft systems. When I try to tell him about things that are routine to me, he stops me. At those times when I really wish I could share with him, I feel so alone.

Inner Feelings

At times, pilots experience feelings that they are uncomfortable expressing to other pilots and, in many instances, to the nonflying public (spouses and other family members included). These may include feelings of doubt, fear, anxiety, embarrassment, anger, and depression. In some cases, such feelings if expressed would (at least in the pilot's mind) be a threat to his employment, social standing (within professional aviation), and identity as a pilot.

When acknowledged by the pilot, these feelings may lead to stress. On the other hand, if they remain suppressed, stress may also develop.

SOCIOCULTURAL FACTORS

Professional aviation, like any industry, cannot function independently of the society of which it is a part. Several influential factors of sociocultural origin tend to impact professional aviation. These include economic factors, laws and regulations, industry trends and changes, current business and management practices, available technology, and political factors.

Each of these elements may account for increased stress for the pilot, as they may be a source of conflict or a source of pressure to conform to more rigid performance standards.

One event—the deregulation of the airline industry in the United States—clearly demonstrates the various sociocultural factors that underlie Pilot Stress Syndrome. This event has been influenced by all of the factors mentioned above and provides a good overview of the sociocultural environment currently existing in commercial aviation.

Airline Deregulation

The Airline Deregulation Act of 1978 has had widespread impact on commercial aviation. Prior to deregulation, economists felt that the airline industry operated as an inefficient cartel. During this period the airlines would base their airfare rates on fluctuations in the economy, rather than on the basis of competitors' rates. When a recession came about and passenger traffic dropped, the Civil Aeronautics Board (CAB) would approve increased fares. When passenger loads increased again, the airlines would compete by offering passengers more inflight services. Any profits made through raised airfares from the recession period would be spent in an attempt to compete with other airlines. This would result in minimal profits and a poor return on investment.

The reason behind airline deregulation was simple. It was believed that by opening the airline industry to competition, many airlines would enter the previously monopolized markets. This would generate capital, while lowering airfares for passengers. In all, it was believed by its proponents that deregulation would be good for the economy.

It was also believed that the deregulation of the airlines would result in a very efficient hub-and-spoke system in which larger airlines would establish operations in larger "hub" cities and the smaller airlines would bring passengers into these hub cities via the smaller "spoke" cities. Such a system would support both the small and large airlines.

The Airline Deregulation Act of 1978 called for a plan enabling air carriers to enter one new route every year until 1981. This would protect the existing market from rapid saturation of carriers. The bill also allowed the CAB to automatically grant operating rights to air carriers that wanted to enter a market being operated by one airline. In addition, the act allowed airlines to decrease their rates by 50% or increase them by 5% without CAB approval. By 1984, the CAB would be disbanded entirely. After that time the Department of Transportation would be given the responsibility of overseeing the airline industry.

Since the introduction of the act, a number of occurrences have taken place in the airline industry. Many of these events were predictable, while many others were not. In an attempt to increase competition and make the industry more profitable, airline deregulation has had both positive and negative effects on the pilot.

To begin with, the hub-and-spoke system has become a major form of operation for the airlines. Though this is not a new method, more and more airlines have adopted it. Its advantages are that it saves fuel and reduces the number of aircraft necessary for passenger use. It also allows passengers to avoid the inconvenience of changing airlines to connect with another flight to travel to another city.

First, a problem with the hub-and-spoke system is that it tends to add more than one hour to the scheduled flight time on one-stop flights. Pilots who fly several one-stop flights during their duty time must contend with more waiting periods between flights than was the case in the past. This can contribute to increased stress and fatigue.

Second, airfares have not risen at the rate that they would have, had the industry not been deregulated. This means that more passengers are able to afford to fly. It accounts for the rapidly expanding airline activity in the United States. It also accounts for such stressors to the pilot as crowded airports, high-density air traffic, increased pressure to meet tighter schedules, and hiring and rapid promotion of pilots with less experience than the airlines required of past flight crews.

Third, nonunionization has become the trend. Since the initiation of the Airline Deregulation Act, several nonunion airlines have entered the market, and some previously unionized carriers have moved toward nonunionized status. This has resulted in considerably less pay for the pilot. For example, nonunion airline captains may earn as little as $30,000 per year, while union captains may make as much as $100,000 flying the same type of aircraft. Those pilots who make less money commonly complain about financial problems:

When I came to work for this airline I knew that I wouldn't make as much money here as I could make at a unionized company. But the reputation here is good and a number of my friends work here. We like it. The only problem is that my wife and I both have to work to pay the bills. This creates a lot of stress between us because she'll soon have to stop working to have the baby.

Concern over lack of job security in nonunionized airlines is also expressed:

I really like my job. I enjoy flying the DC-10. I've been here for ten years, but there's always that lingering thought in the back of my mind that I won't be here for another ten. It's scary.

In addition, airlines have increased the efficiency of labor. Some pilots are required to work forty-hour weeks as compared to the traditional pre-deregulation requirement of fifty hours per month. A 747 captain talked about his experience:

Flying for the airlines is definitely not what it used to be. We are all working harder, longer hours. I'm a senior captain for my airline and I have it a little easier than a lot of the pilots, but I sure don't have it as easy as a lot of the captains before me.

One of the unforeseen problems that has emerged since deregulation first started is that, for the most part, it has failed to bring about new major challengers. The leaders remain. This can be attributed to the cost advantages that the larger airlines have over those that are smaller. The larger companies are controlling terminal facilities and landing slots at congested airports. In addition, they have an advantage over smaller airlines in that they can afford computer reservation systems (CRSs). Ninety percent of all flights booked through travel agents are booked through CRSs.

Another advantage that large airlines have over smaller ones is that they can afford to undercut competitors' fares by increasing prices on less price-sensitive flights. By charging more on very busy flights, profits can be used to outprice competitors. These factors contribute to lack of job security for pilots employed by smaller companies.

A common problem is the merger issue. Major airlines are buying up the small, regional airlines, thus eliminating competition. Airline mergers are becoming a necessary means of survival for many airlines. For the pilot there are advantages and disadvantages to mergers.

One advantage is that the merger can help the purchasing airline grow more rapidly. This expands the airline's operations. More opportunities become available for assignment to a preferred domicile and seniority is gained more rapidly.

Another advantage lies in the expansion of the larger airline's route structure. On some international flights, only two or three airlines are permitted passenger service rights into the countries they service. When an airline merges with another airline that has these limited access rights, the merging airline acquires the rights as part of the deal. For the pilot this may mean there is increased opportunity to partake in international flight, whereas that opportunity might not have existed prior to the merger.

But the positive benefits for the pilot do not come without stress effects. Some of these positive outcomes may mean relocation. Even when the reassignment to a new domicile is a positive move, the pilot will experience the stress that comes with having to relocate.

On the negative side, mergers often bring with them increased conflict between employees from both companies, disputes over how seniority is handled, and scheduling problems that must be worked out. Every airline that merges with another airline experiences a period of readjustment that increases stress for many of the pilots involved. A captain for an airline that was acquired by another major airline observed:

> When our company was purchased by the other airline we were told right out that our pilots would not be considered part of the team. We were told that we would have to wear different uniforms and would be assigned different routes. We wound up with the lousiest routes. It's been real tough and stressful for all of us.

Another captain from another airline that purchased a smaller airline stated:

> Since we acquired the other company, there's been a lot of conflict around here. You know, they took their people and put them on our seniority list. That means that a lot of pilots who have been here for a long time are losing seniority because the other company's pilots have come on board. It's not a fair deal.

Another major concern that has emerged since airline deregulation is for aviation safety. A number of airlines have made it standard practice to defer more maintenance items than they have in the past. One airline has provisions to allow its planes to take off with as many as ninety deferred maintenance items! Needless to say, pilots are very concerned over the decrease in maintenance spending:

> My biggest stressor is my knowledge of the workings of our maintenance department. You wouldn't believe some of the shortcuts they try to take to cut costs. I have refused to fly some of the airplanes we were assigned.

The Airline Deregulation Act of 1978 has caused many pilot concerns to surface. However, as is the case in every type of system, if one part of the system is affected, every other part of that system will also be affected. The aviation system is by no means an exception to this rule. Virtually every sector of aviation has been affected by deregulation. A case in point is the mass increase in traffic density in the skies. This event has introduced new stressors with which every pilot must now contend.

7

Life-Change and Acute Reactive Factors

Throughout life each of us experiences changes that come about naturally. These changes occur at the physiological, intellectual, emotional, family, social, and occupational levels. They are predictable and characterize life events that we all expect to encounter.

When unpredictable and unforeseen events occur, we tend to view them as crisis situations that must be dealt with immediately. These events are known as acute reactive events.

Both life-change and acute reactive events present their own unique stressors of which the pilot should be aware.

LIFE-CHANGE FACTORS

From the time of birth the infant grows and develops. Armed with certain primal instincts, the infant is able to suck, cry, sleep, and eliminate bodily waste materials. In the early period of life this is all that is needed—along with some help from the infant's primary caretaker. This caretaker is usually the infant's mother. She feeds him, clothes him, changes his diapers, and keeps him warm.

Soon the infant learns to crawl, then to walk. He learns to feed himself and talk. In time, he learns that there are other babies in the world just like him. As he grows older he starts to attend school, where his intellectual and social growth become more highly developed. He learns to read, write, draw pictures, paint, and play with others his own age.

Perhaps at some time during early childhood a brother or sister is born. The child, who was his parents' one and only, now becomes one of two children. He may feel rejected by his parents, but for the most part, he gets over it.

In time the child becomes a teenager. Stuck in a young person's body, the teenager finds himself struggling with issues of both the need for dependence and independence from his parents. He gets a job, starts dating, buys a car, graduates from high school, and if he or his parents can afford it, goes off to college. He eventually meets his mate, they marry, and the cycle of life begins again.

Though simplified, the description that I have just provided for one's life is typical. It does not fit everybody's life, but it does provide a foundation for understanding the dynamics of life-change factors that affect all pilots.

Family structures do not always fit the traditional mold. There are currently many variations of family structures: single-parent families, blended families (consisting of a husband, wife, and children from a previous marriage), extended families (husband, wife, children, plus grandparents, aunts, uncles, etc.), gay couples, and dual-career marriages. In many cases the structure of the family may be a major source of stress.

Whatever type of family organization or structure the pilot becomes part of, there are changes over time that emerge which can increase stress.

The predictable changes that we can all expect to encounter are developmental in nature. Regardless of the family structure of the pilot, developmental changes that are unique to his particular structure will occur. Because the majority of pilots live within the traditional family structure, its developmental pattern will be explained. But keep in mind that similar developmental occurrences take place in other structures.

The current trend in family living is toward the traditional nuclear family. The declining divorce rate, the increasing risk of contracting sexually transmitted disease, and the social movement toward stability in relationships are all factors forcing the majority of individuals (pilots included) to seek out and perpetuate the traditional nuclear-family life-style.

In the beginning of this chapter the development of the individual was outlined. If we were to look closely at this individual's growth, we would be able to identify several phases with critical transition points throughout.

One model of family development[1] describes the traditional family life-cycle in eight stages. Each stage is marked by a transitional event that forces the family members to assume new roles.

Marriage marks the first transitional event in the family. The couple must break their emotional and physical ties from their individual families of origin and develop a bond in their new family. The transition to married life can be stressful, as it calls for many adjustments. The

[1]Duvall, E. (1977) *Marriage and Family Development* (5th ed.). New York: Lippincott.

couple must learn to negotiate, communicate, and set rules (some of which are spoken while others are unspoken). These activities tend to be focused on a wide range of subjects, including household chores, sex, money issues, decisions concerning vacations, fair-fighting practices, leisure-time activities, and work-related issues. The average length of time of this stage is two years.

The second stage begins when the first child is born. At this time the family becomes a childbearing family. Stress between the marital couple will generally increase for a number of reasons. First, the husband may feel rejected because his wife is giving much of the attention that he had received prior to the infant's birth, to the new infant. Second, the mother may feel overburdened by the extremely demanding needs of the infant. If she does not feel supported by her husband, she will experience tremendous stress. Many changes take place with the birth of the first child. As a therapist, I feel that the best advice I can give a couple that have just had their first baby is to take care of the child but not forget about the marriage. Intimacy, sharing, communication, and support are important and must be maintained. This second stage of the family life-cycle usually lasts until the child enters preschool, which occurs at the approximate age of thirty months.

When the child enters preschool, the mother may wish to return to work. This may ease the family's financial pressures, but another major stressor may enter the picture: the realization by both parents that the child is becoming less dependent upon them. This often brings up feelings of loss for the parents, and it brings to bear thoughts about the finiteness of the family remaining intact. This stage generally ends when the oldest child reaches six years of age.

When the child enters primary school, the family system once again changes. One or both parents may become actively involved in school activities, and the active participation of the parents may be requested by the child or his or her teacher for assistance with homework. If the child has difficulties in school, stress in the entire family will be experienced. Stage 4 of the family life-cycle usually ends when the oldest child reaches thirteen.

When the child becomes a teenager and experiences puberty, stress will permeate the entire family system. The child will generally become emotionally sensitive and emotionally conflicted. The parents may find this period extremely difficult, as they may feel incompetent as parents, due to an inability to deal with their child's uncontrollable behavior. This stage lasts until the oldest child is approximately twenty years old.

When the first child leaves home, the family system will be characterized as a launching center. Much preparation will take place to help the child prepare to move out of the home before this time. Financial burdens may once again be experienced by the parents. This is particularly true if the parents were unable to prepare for funding of a college education, should they choose to assist the child with college expenses. Stress is also experienced by both parents, who are aware that their child will soon be leaving home. This stage ends when the last child has left home.

Parents of middle age characterize the seventh stage of the family life-cycle. This stage begins when the children have departed the household, leaving an "empty nest" behind. At this time, the couple must face the prospect of having to live with each other until one partner dies. For many adults this is a highly stressful period because it marks a turning point in one's life, where one may encounter an existential crisis. Who am I? Why am I here? Did I do what I should have done? Will I be happy going on for the rest of my life living the way I am, or working in this field? During this period men are most likely to have extramarital affairs and women are most likely to return to college or enter the career world if they have not already done so. However middle-age conflicts are dealt with, they usually pass after much stress. This stage ends at retirement of both partners.

Aging family members marks the eighth and final stage. During this stage, each partner must contend with the realities of life with less income and no work. Spending more time together often creates problems for the couple. They must learn how to put up with each other's inflexible attitudes, habits, and behaviors. Physical ailments, immobility, alienation, and at times apathy can be other sources of stress for the aging couple. This stage ends when both partners have died.

From this overview it becomes clear that life is not without its stressors. As the pilot and his family members move through each of these stages, they will be forced to make adjustments. Some of these changes are welcome while others are not. As with any form of change, resistance may be demonstrated by the pilot. When this occurs, it usually has little impact on the inevitable developmental change, and increases the pilot's stress.

It is true that the stages outlined here do not necessarily apply to families that do not remain intact. Divorce, death of a spouse, or other events can alter the life-cycle. However, awareness of the existence of developmental stages affecting one's family can be helpful to the pilot regardless of his family structure. By looking at the obvious predictable changes that he can expect to occur throughout his life, the pilot can take preparatory steps to minimize stress effects as these events are encountered.

Life change can also occur in the pilot's occupational life. Events such as being hired by a company or being selected for military flight school, pilot training, route assignment, domicile assignment, relocation, transition and upgrade training, and job promotion are developmental stages with which pilots must cope.

It is important for the pilot to be aware that domestic and occupational life-change events are interactional. The pilot cannot take action in one area without positively or negatively affecting the other. A corporate pilot addressed this connection:

> Every time I moved through each of the developmental stages of the family life-cycle . . . I did experience stress. I found that I couldn't separate my work and home issues. I couldn't help but bring my domestic stress into the cockpit and vice versa.

If family members work cooperatively in an effort to meet the various crisis events that occur in the developmental life-cycle of the family, family life will be rewarding and satisfying. With this strong domestic foundation, overall stress coping for the pilot will be enhanced.

ACUTE REACTIVE FACTORS

Acute reactive factors may be defined as those situations requiring immediate action to be taken in order to prevent further escalation of a problem that may result in some form of loss, damage, or destruction. These situations include inflight emergencies, occupational crises, and personal-life crises.

Inflight Emergencies

Loss, damage, or destruction, when discussed in the context of inflight emergencies, applies to the aircraft, its crew, and its passengers. It is how emergencies are handled, especially in flight, that will determine the final outcome. If any one or more factors that underlie Pilot Stress Syndrome are present in great enough magnitude, the outcome will be disastrous, as evidenced by the following National Transportation Safety Board synopses denoting probable cause in a number of aircraft accidents:

. . . the flight crew's (a) disregard for prescribed procedures for monitoring and controlling of airspeed during the final stages of the approach, (b) decision to continue the landing rather than execute a missed approach, and (c) overreliance on the autothrottle speed control system which had a history of recent malfunctioning.[2]

. . . the captain's decision to accept and maintain an excessive airspeed derived from the autothrottle speed control system during the landing approach which caused the airplane to land about 2,800 feet beyond the runway's displaced threshold.[3]

. . . the flight crew's decision to initiate and continue the approach into a cumulonimbus cloud which they observed to contain visible lightning. . . .[4]

[2]National Transportation Safety Board. (1984) *Aircraft Accident Report: Scandinavian Airlines System Flight 901.* Washington, D.C.: NTSB/AAR-84/15-PB84-910415.

[3]National Transportation Safety Board. (1985) *Aircraft Accident Report: World Airways, Inc., Flight 30H.* Washington, D.C.: NTSB/AAR-85/06-PB85-91046.

[4]National Transportation Safety Board. (1986) *Aircraft Accident Report: Delta Airlines, Inc.* Washington, D.C.: NTSB/AAR-86/05-PB86-910406.

. . . the captain's continuation of an unstabilized approach which resulted in a descent below glideslope . . . and the captain's acceptance of a nonstandard air-traffic-control radar vector resulting in an excessive intercept with the localizer.[5]

Though the National Transportation Safety Board did not specifically refer to Pilot Stress Syndrome in these aircraft accident statements, at least some degree of causation should be suspected based on the evidence presented thus far in this book.

Occupational Crisis

The relative instability of a career in professional aviation is well known among pilots. Economic factors, loss of license, medical problems, or stress may pose a threat to job security, leading to occupational crisis. As with other acute reactive situations, the pilot must take immediate action when crisis occurs. In this case, action must be taken to prevent loss or damage to the pilot's job. A veteran airline pilot experienced such a crisis:

It was really looking like I was going to lose my medical certificate. The stress I was experiencing was so bad that I was a mess. I was up to two packs of cigarettes a day, my weight was getting up there, and something showed up on my EKG. I knew I had to clean up my act or I'd be out of a job. So I went on a diet, started exercising, entered a program to stop smoking, and got some counseling in order to deal with my stress. That was last year. I'm glad I handled my problems. I feel great now.

[5]National Transportation Safety Board. (1986) *Aircraft Accident Report: Bar Harbor Airlines Flight 1808.* Washington, D.C.: NTSB/AAR-86/06-PB86-910408.

Other occupational crisis situations include threat of loss of position or status, pay, or esteem among peers and co-workers:

> When I failed to pass my company's sim check I was real worried that all of the other pilots would look down on me. I felt like I had lost face. I had to pass the second time around.

Personal-Life Crisis

Any crisis event that occurs in the pilot's personal life qualifies as a personal-life crisis. Death of a friend is one such event that can create high levels of stress for the pilot. This is especially true if the friend's death occurred while flying an aircraft. It forces the pilot to face the realities of the dangers that exist in aviation. Another personal-life crisis event that the pilot may experience is the death of his spouse. This is a major stressor for the pilot, as immediate action must be taken to meet the demands of the sudden role changes that invariably take place. The same is true for the death of any family member. A corporate first officer whose husband had died six months prior to my interview with her shared her experience:

> When Seth died suddenly in a car crash I felt like my world had crumbled. I had to take charge in areas that Seth had been the master of. I also had to handle the finances, funeral arrangements, selling of our house, and I was left with a child to raise. On top of this, I was very emotional for the first few months. I still am at times, but thank goodness I had the support I needed from my friends.

Personal-life crisis events are characterized by any acute reactive situation where one's basic personal or social needs are threatened with potential loss, damage, or destruction. These include physiological, safety, love, esteem, and actualization needs. In addition to death of a friend, spouse, or other family member, several other threats exist. They include sudden illness of a family member, loss of income, financial difficulties, legal problems, a traffic accident, family automobile or other property problems, crime victimization, a problem teenager, domestic disputes, discovery of infidelity, unplanned pregnancy, and marital separation and divorce.

Once an acute reactive situation of any kind has terminated, the natural stress response should diminish, eventually to the point of resolution. If resolution fails to come about or if it comes about too slowly, continued stress will be experienced by the pilot and those around him. This puts additional strain on the pilot, which may affect his mental and physical functioning. Recognition of abnormal resolution can help the pilot, his friends, or family members determine if and when professional assistance should be sought.

Some of the indications of unresolved acute reactive experience include depression; persistent anxiety; ineffective stress coping; withdrawal; isolation; paranoid behavior; agitation; excessive sleep or insomnia; nightmares; excessive loss or gain in weight since the incident; poor flight performance; inappropriate emotional expression (such as laughing when sad events are discussed); memory loss; physical ailments; numbness; paralysis; compulsive behavior (such as gambling or going on spending sprees); feelings of helplessness or hopelessness; increased drinking, smoking, or drug use; scattered thinking; phobic (extreme fear) reactions; excessive emotionality; and general irritability. These signs represent red flags that indicate something is wrong. The presence of any of these reactions since the trauma should be a warning to the pilot that he may not be safe to fly aircraft. He should discuss his problems with his AME, who can refer him to a professional trained to help individuals resolve their traumatic experiences.

Post-traumatic Stress Disorder

For some pilots, unresolved trauma may lead to Post-traumatic Stress Disorder. This is a disorder that tends to affect individuals who are exposed to distressing events that lie outside the range of usual human experience.

The stressors leading to Post-traumatic Stress Disorder may involve catastrophic events such as a plane crash, serious threat of harm to one's self or others, sudden destruction of property, or the witnessing of another's death. Crime and terrorism are two other stressors that can lead to Post-traumatic Stress Disorder.

The pilot may experience the traumatic event alone or with others. In the latter case, entire flight crews have been known to experience this disorder.

After the trauma has taken place, it may be reexperienced. This can occur through intrusive, repetitive thoughts or dreams about the event. These are usually vivid and cause the pilot a great degree of anxiety. They may also cause extreme phobic reactions. In rare instances the pilot may experience dissociative states that may last from a few seconds to several hours, during which he relives the trauma. These states are commonly referred to as flashbacks.

The pilot may attempt to avoid situations that remind him of the trauma in order to avoid the possibility of being involved in a similar traumatic event.

Detachment from other people is not uncommon after

the trauma. Pilots who have experienced Post-traumatic Stress Disorder have commonly reported a feeling of emotional numbness. They become less involved socially, intimately, and sexually. They may also report loss of interest in activities that they found enjoyable prior to the trauma.

After the trauma, the pilot may become overly alert and cautious. He may find himself very "edgy," and may react to noises around him with a startle reaction. Typically, these pilots report having problems sleeping. Irritability and emotional outbursts are also common.

A 747 second officer described the effects of his Post-traumatic Stress on his career:

> I was assigned to the San Francisco–Boston run. It was a cold, windy night at SFO and the weather en route wasn't going to be good. I knew it. We'd be flying through some mean weather just outside of SFO and we weren't going to clear it until we were in the mid-twenties. Right out of ten, after departure, we hit the worst turbulence I had ever experienced in my life. We experienced structural damage, so we had to return to home base. The experience was so terrifying for all of us [the entire flight crew] that every time I experience anything approaching even moderate turbulence I start to panic. This incident happened last year and my anxiety appears to be getting worse, not better. It's gotten to the point where I don't want to fly anymore.

The copilot of a C-130 told of his personal experience:

> Immediately following the plane crash, my life seemed to slow down. I didn't want to go near another airplane and I found it hard to concentrate. I couldn't sleep at night, and the dreams—they kept coming. No matter what I did to stop them, I kept having them.

Recognition of the fact that the pilot may be affected by Post-traumatic Stress Disorder is an important first step in helping him deal with this crippling and painful problem.

The second step involves the pilot's willingness to seek professional assistance. There is no reason for the pilot to carry the pain of trauma around with him for the rest of his life. Counseling is quite often effective in helping the pilot resolve his suffering.

Finally, the issue of loss must be addressed. Loss, whether it occurs through death, divorce, or separation, can be a painful and enduring experience for the pilot. It is difficult to live and function normally when we have lost somebody whom we love. Often it feels as though we have lost a part of ourselves—and, in reality, we have lost an important part of our life.

There are some typical stages that most people move through when they are grieving the loss of a loved one. These stages are presented here so that you can recognize them in yourself or others. All major losses should be seriously considered as major stressors for the pilot, and when they are experienced, I recommend taking some time off from flying so that healing can take place.

The first stage of loss is characterized by denial and isolation. The pilot experiencing this stage will find it difficult to accept the loss that will occur (as in a loved one dying) or has occurred. He may try to continue with his flight duties as if nothing is happening. This pilot may isolate himself from others either physically or emotionally.

Anger characterizes the second stage of loss. Feelings of hostility and resentment are not uncommonly experienced during the anger stage. The anger may center around unfinished business, unattained goals, and extreme frustration. The pilot may direct his anger at other family members, friends, co-workers, or the medical team.

Once anger has subsided, the pilot will enter the bargaining stage. Since there is no rational way out of the loss, irrational approaches are used. The pilot may attempt to bargain with God, the physician, or anybody whom he feels can keep the loss from occurring (if it has not actually taken place yet). If it has occurred, bargaining may be directed toward helping the lost loved one get to a place where he or she will be content. It may also be used in an attempt to help the pilot resolve the pain of the loss.

Depression, the next stage, is usually accompanied by feelings of guilt, sorrow, and shame. The grief experienced by the pilot during this stage should be expressed. It is an important step toward acceptance, which is the final stage of loss.

Acceptance is characterized by an inner sense of calmness. The pilot who has accepted his loss has let go of his pain and is ready to move on with his life.

When loss is experienced, support from others is often helpful. Should the pilot experience complications with his grief process, he can become stuck in one of these stages. If this is experienced, counseling can be of help.

8

*Professional Pilots
Speak on Stress*

The pilot. He's the vital link in the aviation system. His job is to control the multimillion-dollar machines that are owned by the airlines, corporations, and governments of the world. He spends many years training and honing his skills in hopes of advancing to the left seat. His job is demanding and inherently stressful. He must not only fly the airplane, but he is responsible for balancing the sometimes thin line between safety and efficiency. Where a safety margin does not exist, he creates one. He must keep up with current technology, being ever so aware of the fact that any gap in knowledge could mean the difference between life and death. These people who are entrusted with the lives of millions of passengers each year are special. Their dedication, self-discipline, intelligence, skill, and expertise account for the safety record that, surprisingly, exists in the aviation system. Given that a slight numerical misinterpretation, the movement of a wrong control, or one of many possible errors can cause tragedy, it is amazing how aviation continues to be the safest mode of transportation today. The incredible safety record is attributed, to a great degree, to the pilot.

Envied by many who are not trained to fly, the pilot loves his job. For most pilots, aviation seems to be an incurable addiction. But when we come to understand the pilot's psyche, we realize that his bond with aviation is much stronger than the addictive bond many people think pilots are prisoners of. His bond exists within the roots of his identity. For aviation is his identity.

The pilot is often misunderstood by his nonflying family and friends. The haven of his home can only partially provide him with the support he needs when experiencing pilot stress. During those times when he is able to, he turns to his professional peers. But there are other times when even his peers cannot be of help because he knows that if he communicates his deepest feelings about his anxieties he might become an outcast, rejected not because he has been labeled by his peers as ill or broken in some way, but because his own pain may strike a reminder of the stress that many pilots unconsciously experience. The result is suppression and denial of the stress that the pilot feels.

Professional pilots recognize, perhaps more than anybody else, the presence of stress in their jobs. They also realize that they must function well in the cockpit in spite of the vast number of stressors with which they are faced.

I interviewed four pilots to see what they had to say about the stress associated with their jobs. These pilots were candid and welcomed the opportunity to speak to their professional aviation colleagues. Three of the pilots interviewed are currently flying as airline pilots. The fourth is a corporate pilot. Three of the four are married and have children, and all have been involved in professional aviation for many years. The names of these pilots, their companies, and any information that would lead to their identities have been changed so they could speak freely.

Garrett was the first of the four pilots I interviewed for this chapter. He is thirty-three years old, is married and has two daughters, ages four and six. He is currently a first officer assigned to the MD-80 and works for a major air carrier. He is based in the Midwest and has been employed by his airline for two years.

Lee, a forty-three-year-old second officer, is assigned to the L-1011. He is based on the West Coast and works for a major airline that has merged with another air carrier. He has been employed by his company for almost twelve years. He is married and has two daughters, ages five and eight.

Andrea, age thirty-six, is a captain assigned to the B-737. She is single and is based on the East Coast. She works for a major airline and has been employed with her company for eight years.

Mark, the corporate pilot whom I interviewed, is thirty-six years old. He flies as a King Air 300 captain. He has been with his company for three months, and has been a professional pilot since 1976. He is married, has two sons, ages four and eleven, and a daughter, age eight.

The first question I asked each of the pilots was, "What would you say your strengths and weaknesses are as a person?"

Garrett felt he had two strengths and one weakness:

I feel that my first strength is my ability to get along well with all kinds of people from different backgrounds. The second is my firmness on issues.

The one weakness that I have been able to identify is that sometimes I think I'm too nice a guy. If I don't agree with something somebody says, I don't make an issue of it right away. I do this to keep the conversation going. I don't have that attitude at work though. When I'm on the job I'm a different person. I'll speak up right away if somebody says or does something I disagree with.

Lee felt that his strength has been the major cause for his remaining in aviation for many years:

> My strength is discipline. You have to have discipline to stay in aviation for as long as I have. I developed discipline over the years, and this is what has helped me to stick with aviation.

Conversely, Lee also sees this is as weakness:

> [Laughing]: My weakness is my stupidity to stay with it. It's the typical pilot syndrome—buy high, sell low, and make it up in volume.

Lee's cost/benefit perspective is a consideration that is held in the consciousness of many pilots. In most cases the financial rewards of flying are few compared with other occupations. This is a source of stress for many pilots.

Andrea felt that her major strengths centered around her ability to work well with her co-workers and her ability to adapt:

> I really love crew coordination. I learned it early on when I flew as a corporate pilot. I've always been able to get along well with those I work with. When things run smoothly because my first officer and I are communicating well, I feel elated. My adaptability would have to be my second strongest point. You have to be adaptable to be a safe airline captain.
>
> I have two weaknesses that I have to work on. The first is my self-criticalness. I beat myself up a lot. I know I can't be perfect, but somehow I've got it in my mind that I have to be. My other weakness is that I am often overly judgmental of other pilots. If they're a little slow on the radio, or they delay the rest of us when we're trying to get into the airport, I sometimes come unglued. My first officer laughs about it. He tells me that when I yell at the

other pilots they can't hear me. One day he reached into a duffel bag that he brought aboard and pulled out a megaphone and said, "try this." I guess the yelling is my way of reducing my stress.

Mark had difficulty answering the question at first:

You know, that's a tough one. I haven't given this much thought. [After a little stumbling, the answer came to him very clearly. It was as if he had been aware of it all along]: My strong points are that I like working with other people. I want people contact. In this field I deal with everybody. I deal with the airplane owner, the caterers, the passengers, maintenance people, fuelers, controllers—everybody.

As far as aviation goes, my strong points lie in my ability to follow procedures well and adapt to different situations. I'm also always on time when it comes to aviation.

On the weak side, I am not as detailed as I should be when it comes to paperwork. I also find that I'm rarely on time in my personal life. I'm much more carefree when it comes to nonflying activities. I don't know why that's so.

Mark was the second pilot to mention the existence of a double standard between his personal- and professional-life behavior. This is not uncommon among pilots. They generally possess a double identity. One is the aviation-related identity, which meets the demands for more rigid and precise behavior required of the pilot; and the other is the less rigid identity that he experiences away from the aviation environment.

In my next question, I asked these pilots to describe their typical schedules.

Garrett said that he isn't flying much right now:

I'm on reserve. Right now I'm flying about nine days a month. It's stressful sitting around waiting. I want to fly more. I would gladly trade vacation time to fly. I sit around the house hoping that I'll get a phone call to come in and fly, and when I'm on the phone with somebody or when I leave the house, I have my pager on.

Lee feels that his schedule is too demanding:

I fly from [the West Coast] to Hawaii. I arrive in Honolulu at 10:00 P.M., which is the equivalent of about midnight our [West Coast] body time. I leave Honolulu at 10:00 P.M. the next evening and arrive on the West Coast at 6:00 A.M. local time. Then I have to leave for Honolulu again at 10:00 P.M. the same day and repeat the cycle. I do this five days a week. For most pilots flying from midnight to sunup, the body doesn't adjust very well. As I get older I find it harder to adjust to these sleep schedules. During the weekdays when the kids are gone I can sleep pretty well, but when they're home and it's noisy I find it difficult to catch up on my sleep.

Lee's schedule is complicated by the jet-lag effects he experiences. He is also concerned about the drive from the airport to his home:

When I arrive at my domicile I have another major stressor to deal with. That is the rush-hour traffic that I have to battle to get home.

Andrea also feels that her schedule is demanding:

My schedule changes from month to month. Being that I am flying a short-range airplane, I run a lot of the commuter flights up and down the East Coast. In one eight-hour day I can land at and take off from more cities than you can imagine. Out here we get some pretty bad weather. That makes it tougher. On some days every approach I make has to be made down to minimums. By the end of the day I'm thoroughly exhausted. I can fly as many as thirty hours per week.

Mark's schedule is different:

I'm on call twenty-four hours a day. I fly about twenty-five hours per month for the company and I try to schedule about ten hours of charter work each month. The longest trip that I've ever taken lasted two weeks. Once a year I am away for one week. Four-day trips are the longest I can stand being away from home. This is one of the reasons why I like the King Air. Most of my trips are in the local area. I've only been averaging one night per week away from home. The lack of predictability of my schedule is a source of stress for me.

Each pilot indicated that his schedule was stressful. I've observed that whether a pilot's schedule is too demanding or too slow, stress presents itself. Many pilots argue that the boredom of waiting around to fly can be as stressful as flying too much. This led to my next question: "What do you like most about your job?"

Garrett was enthusiastic with his response:

I love my job. It's all I ever dreamed it would be, plus some. What do I like most about my job? The travel and the challenge. I enjoy it when I've just flown and I've done a great job. Every time I fly I have to prove myself.

"Why is that?" I asked.

It's something inside me that makes me want to experience the accomplishment. It's the challenge. When I fly I feel alive.

The need to prove oneself is not uncommon among pilots. When the pilot meets the challenge placed on him by himself, he feels a sense of euphoria. But when he doesn't live up to his standards of excellence, he may feel demoralized. Both of these outcomes result in stress. Meeting the challenge results in positive stress, while failure to meet the challenge results in negative stress.

Lee is happy with the free time his job provides:

> I like the time off. My job allows me to be home a lot with my wife and the kids. I have two full weekends off per month. I get more time with my family than most people who have a 9-to-5 schedule.

Andrea's response was closely tied into her identity:

> My job allows me to express myself in ways that other jobs wouldn't. When I enter the cockpit I feel great. I'm at home. You know, as I'm talking to you about this I'm realizing that I can't separate who I am from my job. It's as though I don't feel settled until I'm behind the controls of an airplane. Yeah—I feel less stress when I'm on the job than when I'm away from it. I guess the job provides me with structure that I can't find outside the world of aviation. That's the real plus of my work.

Andrea's need for structure is a deeply ingrained personality need that her job fulfills. She identifies so strongly with the fulfillment of this need which aviation provides, that she feels at home when in the aviation environment. Stress is experienced when she doesn't have this structure in her life.

Mark's response to this question was clear and concise:

> I enjoy my job because I do it well and it's something I enjoy doing. The job provides me with independence. It's the next-best thing to owning my own business. It's like I'm my own boss.

Every one of these pilots' responses had one thing in common—they realized that the job provided them with a sense of freedom. None of the pilots felt like they were prisoners of their work.

The least enjoyable aspects of their jobs were addressed next.

Garrett didn't particularly like the impact of automation on his work:

> They're taking the pilot out of the job of piloting aircraft. A lot of responsibility and decision making is being made by gate agents and management. Decisions are being taken away from the flight crews. When we arrive at the airplane, the flight plan is already put into the computer. Management stresses using the advanced computerized systems. Piloting is moving toward automation. Pilots are now flying by pushing buttons and turning knobs. In my opinion the machines increase workload. We have to monitor them very closely. When it comes down to it, if the autopilot goes through 35,000 feet they will violate the pilot, not the machine. I had to laugh when I saw a company bulletin that told the pilots that in comparison to the older onboard computer, the new computer will help you experience "fewer altitude excursions." This means that it won't screw up as much, but it will still screw up. Professional pilots don't trust automation. They use it and monitor it closely. The pilot can easily develop a false sense of security with the system.

The issue of automation was recognized by Garrett as a potential source of stress for the pilot. He went on:

> My airline is very automated. We have a rule book that tells us what we can and can't do, and when we can and can't do it. In a sense they want us to be robots. They go as far as telling the pilots what terminology to use when using the radios. Onboard we have a computer

that transmits engine-performance data periodically throughout the flight. The information is sent via ground-based telephone lines to a central location where aircraft performance is monitored. Management can look at the performance data and determine if we did what we should have been doing at particular periods during the flight. Many of us feel like we're being watched all the time. It can be very stressful.

Lee felt that going away for training is the least enjoyable aspect of his job:

When we go to the Flight Training Center it's extremely stressful. During my initial training on the L-1011 I was back there for six weeks. A lot of the guys have nervous breakdowns there. If you don't believe me, just ask the drivers who shuttle you between the hotels and the training center. Boy, do they have stories they can tell you about stress. In one month I had seven sims. With the first six, I got six orals, and the last sim was the check ride.

"What happens when a pilot takes a sim check and doesn't pass it?" I asked.

We have a good company. They stand by their people. They'll send you through again if you have a good attitude.

"What do you mean by a 'good attitude'? How do they determine that?"

Well, if they see that you're really trying and you want to do a good job, the instructors will bend over backwards to help you. Some of the instructors will even voluntarily come in on their day off to help a pilot who is having a lot of trouble. This is a far cry from the airlines that will let you go if you blow a check ride.

Andrea's experience was different. She was not happy with the way her company treats their employees.

> We walk on eggshells in our company. The management doesn't really take care of us. When my airline decided to cut expenses, flight-crew salaries and benefits were among the first to be hit. I know I'm young and I don't have to worry as much about it as the older pilots, but our company's retirement plan is far from adequate. I figure I'll be here another year before I leave. I want to get some more left-seat experience under my belt. Then I'll move on. When a company doesn't take care of it employees they don't deserve the best. They get what they're paying for and I'm not worth that little.

Complaints of this type echo through my psychotherapy office all the time. Pilots who feel they are not being adequately supported both economically and emotionally are generally very angry and very stressed. Feeling as though they are being taken advantage of, these pilots tend to either leave their companies for greener pastures or resign themselves to a life of economic difficulties. Some pilots' wives help them financially. Where the company does not provide emotional support, family and friends do. Andrea continued:

> I think corporate greed is at the root of all of this. I know things are financially tight in the industry, but most airline CEOs think in terms of rapid return on their investments. They cut pilot wages and benefits and wind up with a lot of stressed-out pilots because we can't afford to pay our bills. The turnover is high, so they have to spend a lot more in training costs. Stress creates a safety risk. If one of us crashes an airplane, the airline loses their shirt. And all of those lives. It doesn't make sense.

Mark felt that the least enjoyable aspect of his job was what he referred to as the "common place theory."

> I used to like my job for the travel. Now that doesn't turn me on very much.

"What changed that for you?" I asked.

> I think it's the common place theory. You go to the same place time and time again. After a while you get revolted by hotel rooms. Another aspect of my job that is not enjoyable is the instability of corporate flying. I have never stayed with a single company for more than three years before the company let go of the airplane. Also, I'm thirty-six years old with a family and a mortgage payment. I take physicals every six months. At any time I can get blown out of the saddle.

I was interested in knowing what fears these pilots had that were associated with flying.

Garrett had to think about the question for a while before he could provide his answers:

> I can't really identify a fear. Thunderstorms, maybe—well, I can't say it's a fear because I stay away from them. If I have something that I fear I try to analyze it and my knowledge of it helps me to overcome it. I guess if I had one, it would be transatlantic flight in a two-engine plane.

Lee's response was brief:

> Most guys say their biggest fear is having their medical certificate taken away from them. This and inflight structural failure are my two fears.

Andrea's fears were similar:

> I can't bear the thought of being grounded. I take care of my body so that I won't be grounded because of a

medical cause. I also fear having problems with the airplane. Mechanical problems in flight don't occur often, but when they do they can be pretty serious.

Mark talked about his fears and how he deals with them:

My biggest fear is being involved in a situation that I have no control over. I find that midair collisions, structural failures, and bad weather are some of the things that I may have very little control of.

I rely on basic procedures when I am faced with things that otherwise would be out of my control. If you don't have something to revert to when you are real scared, the panic can be very consuming. I don't let that happen.

After hearing each pilot respond to the previous questions, I asked, "What is the most stressful part of your job?"

Garrett addressed two major stressors:

One of the things that can cause stress is the relationship you have with the other guy. If you're working with a guy who goes by the book and he messes up, you know something's wrong. If he doesn't follow procedures by the book it creates stress. You are put in the position of jumping on the other guy. This can be very stressful.

Some guys try to be intimidating. If they know you're new to the airplane they try to take advantage of you in one way or another. I've also flown with some captains who were overly critical. They try to teach you how to fly the airplane their way when your way may be more effective. I don't like it when they do that—heck, I've got seven thousand hours. I know how to fly an airplane. But I don't let it destroy my relationship with him. I have to work with the guy for three days, and I keep in mind the motto of our company's CRM program, which is to listen to what the other guy has to say because he might be telling you something important.

Another major source of stress is flying in highly dense traffic. I'm used to that because I did all of my flying on the West Coast before I was hired by [my airline]. But I find that when I fly to the West Coast with some captains, they become very anxious. They often become preoccupied with traffic that isn't even a factor. I see some of these captains with their eyes outside the airplane too much—so much so that they aren't concentrating on flying the airplane. When I see a captain do this I feel stress. I have to put my eyes inside the cockpit more to cover for him.

There are those times when regular procedures are stressful. An example of this is the loop departure out of San Jose. There are altitude restrictions and heading changes that have to be made within a relatively short time frame. This keeps us real busy. There was one crew that was doing this particular departure one day when the flight attendant called the cockpit to inform the crew that they smelled smoke in the cabin. Talk about stress.

Lee felt that his schedule was his major source of stress:

The back side of the clock is my primary source of stress. It's real tough.

Andrea's financial problems accounted for the majority of her stress:

As I said, things aren't as good as they should be. It's hard to get along sometimes. As a captain I make more money than first and second officers, but my cost of living is higher too. I have to make mortgage payments. I'm also trying to pay off some debts that I have incurred over the years.

The last question I asked my interviewees was, "How do you manage your stress?" The answers were both creative and interesting.

Garrett:

> My buddy and I bought radio-controlled cars. We go out to the parking lot and play demolition derby and laugh like kids. [Looking at his broken car]: This happened last night. I have to have it fixed. It's expensive, but we really get rid of a lot of tension. My neighbors know what I do for a living. They must think I'm crazy when they see me playing with the cars. We also exercise. That helps a lot.

Lee has a more expensive hobby:

> I have my compressor and tools out in the garage. I'm restoring an old car. I also go out and play tennis.

Andrea loves to sail:

> A friend of mine and I own a sailboat. We take it out as often as we can. The cold water and the smell of salt in the air is calming.
>
> I'm not much for physical exercise, but I take walks to keep myself fit. I prefer to meditate rather than exercise.

Mark:

> Again, I think that my reliance on basic procedures helps me to cope with stress. They give me something to fall back on when the going gets rough.

Having interviewed these pilots, I felt that it would be appropriate to give each an opportunity to make a closing comment.

Garrett:

> I think pilots should be more aware of the effects of stress and deal with these effects.

Lee:

I'm glad that this book is coming out. We've needed this kind of information for a long time. Maybe somebody in administration will read it. Pilots should manage their stress. You always do things better if you are rested. You must relax your mind.

Andrea:

I'd like to tell my peers and everybody involved in aviation that I chose to make my thoughts public because I love aviation. It's a great occupation to be involved in. I'd like to see things improve so that we can all enjoy our profession. I think that stress management for the pilot is important and I want to know more about it.

Mark:

I'd like to see better flight training for the corporate pilot. Many of us have to learn to fly in high-altitude environments and weather the hard way. That means with paying passengers aboard. Professional pilot training has to be upgraded so that those in corporate aviation are more knowledgeable. This would be a major step toward the management of pilot stress.

I would also like to know that other pilots experience the same things that I do, so that I don't feel that I'm strange. This is one of the reasons why a book like this is important. If we all communicate our thoughts and feelings more openly, we'll face the issues that lead to pilot stress and start dealing with them.

Now that you have read some of the thoughts that pilots have on stress, I hope that your own thinking process has begun. Each of us has to look within himself to see where our stressors lie so that we can deal with them.

II

MANAGING
PILOT STRESS

9

Measuring Pilot Stress

Before any problem can be solved it must first be identified as a problem. You must learn as much about it as you can, then take steps to solve it.

Pilot stress must be handled in the same manner if effective stress management is to take place. You must first identify your stress. Then you must learn as much as you possibly can about the sources and effects of your stress. Once you have done this, you will be more able to direct your stress-management activities so that they will make the biggest impact.

In this chapter, you will find some tools that will help you to better identify and understand your stress. They are simple to use. Just follow the instructions.

As you use these tools, bear in mind that they can, at best, be only rough measures of your stress. No measurement device can be more accurate than your own knowledge of the presence of one or more stressors in your life. If you are aware of a source of stress, deal with it, regardless of what the measurement tool says. Use the tool as a road sign to point the way, but be aware of other stressors that the tool might not be sensitive enough to detect.

The measurement tools outlined in this book are:

1. *The Pilot Stress Inventory*—This inventory can help you to determine the categories of stressors that most adversely affect you. A numerical rating scale is presented to help illustrate the degree of stress present.

2. *The Stress Dynamics Scale*—This scale can be used to determine the characteristics of a particular stressor that may be affecting you most. This scale is also used to derive the Nonfunctioning Stress Profile (NSP) and the Maximum Functioning Stress Profile (MFSP). Both are outlined in Chapter 2. The Stress Dynamics Scale will be elaborated on in this chapter.

After you have completed the Pilot Stress Inventory, add the total points for each category of stressors (see Table 9–1). Then divide by 5. For example, let's say you have 21 points for the "Physiological Factors" category. Divide that number by 5. Your total score is 4.2 points. If the total score is any fraction above a number, round it off to the next higher number. In this case your score would be 5.

Now compare each of the total scores to the scale below:

1. Very low
2. Slight
3. Moderate
4. Considerable
5. Extreme

By using this scale you will be able to determine which categories of stressors tend to create the greatest degree of stress for you.

You can also determine your overall stress level by adding all of the total scores and dividing that number by 10. For example, let's say that the sum of a pilot's total scores is 35 points. Divide that number by 10 and the

The Pilot Stress Inventory

In each question below you are to indicate what your normal attitude, behavior, or experience is:

1 = Rarely (less than 10% of the time)
2 = Occasionally (about 30% of the time)
3 = Sometimes (about 50% of the time)
4 = Frequently (about 70% of the time)
5 = Usually (more than 90% of the time)

_____ 1. I have persistent, recurring thoughts or worries.

_____ 2. I become mentally overloaded.

_____ 3. My attention becomes fixated on objects or events while I'm in the cockpit.

_____ 4. I tend to overlook things.

_____ 5. My flights terminate between 5:00 A.M. and 9:30 A.M.

_____ 6. I have difficulty recalling important information.

_____ 7. I have vivid dreams at night.

_____ 8. I am easily reminded of past events when stressful things occur in the present.

_____ 9. I am very emotional.

_____ 10. I find myself reacting emotionally in situations where logical thinking would be more helpful.

_____ 11. I do not tolerate my personal imperfections very well.

_____ 12. My work doesn't give me the excitement that I need.

_____ 13. I avoid revealing my true feelings to co-workers.

_____ 14. I am highly driven and ambitious.

_____ 15. I am self-critical.

_____ 16. I experience emotional tension.

_____ 17. I have a physical problem or illness.

_____ 18. I have one or more fears that I think about.

_____ 19. I have conflicts with family members or co-workers.

_____ 20. I have a negative attitude.

_____ 21. I don't eat a proper diet.

_____ 22. I smoke, overeat, or drink.

_____ 23. I experience fatigue.

_____ 24. I become excited.

_____ 25. I have difficulty falling asleep or remaining asleep.

_____ 26. I have either too little or too much work to do on the job.

_____ 27. I have poor relations on the job.

_____ 28. I tend to bring my work-related issues home with me.

_____ 29. I am not satisfied with my job.

_____ 30. I fly in adverse weather.

_____ 31. I feel emotionally or physically isolated from my family or friends.

_____ 32. I don't feel a sense of comraderie with my co-workers.

_____ 33. I find it difficult to express doubt, fear, anxiety, embarrassment, or anger to my spouse or family members.

_____ 34. I suppress my feelings.

_____ 35. When I take tests I become very nervous.

_____ 36. I worry about job instability.

_____ 37. I have financial problems.

_____ 38. My work schedule is too demanding.

_____ 39. My company defers maintenance items.

_____ 40. Pilots who work for my company don't get along well with management.

_____ 41. I experience stress from events in my family life.

_____ 42. I experience stress from events in my professional life.

_____ 43. I am burdened by responsibilities in either my personal or professional life.

_____ 44. I don't socialize.

_____ 45. I don't exercise.

_____ 46. I have had an occupational crisis within the last year.

_____ 47. I feel threatened by loss of pay.

_____ 48. I have experienced a personal-life crisis within the last year.

_____ 49. I have recurring thoughts or recurring dreams about a crisis that has occurred at some time in my life.

_____ 50. I grieve over a loved one whom I lost through death, divorce, breakup, or separation.

Table 9–1

Questions	Category of Stressors	Points ÷ 5 = Total
1–5	Conscious Factors	_____ ÷ 5 = _____
6–10	Unconscious Factors	_____ ÷ 5 = _____
11–15	Personality Factors	_____ ÷ 5 = _____
16–20	Psychological Factors	_____ ÷ 5 = _____
21–25	Physiological Factors	_____ ÷ 5 = _____
26–30	Environmental Factors	_____ ÷ 5 = _____
31–35	Experiential Factors	_____ ÷ 5 = _____
36–40	Sociocultural Factors	_____ ÷ 5 = _____
41–45	Life-Change Factors	_____ ÷ 5 = _____
46–50	Acute Reactive Factors	_____ ÷ 5 = _____

answer becomes 3.5. Again, round the number up to the next higher number and you get an overall stress score of 4 points.

When we compare the overall stress score to the scale above, we find that this pilot is experiencing "considerable" stress.

Once you have become aware that you are experiencing high levels of stress in one or more of the categories of stressors depicted on the Pilot Stress Inventory, you can work toward identifying the specific source of your stress. When the source is identified, you can use the Pilot Stress Profile (outlined in Chapter 2) to see how the stressor is affecting your life. Is its intensity too high? Does its quality rate as being very significant? Is your exposure to the stressor too frequent? These are questions that can be answered by using the Stress Dynamics Scale.

To understand the level of severity of each of the characteristics of a stressor on the Stress Dynamics Scale, you can use the following scoring system:

1 = Minimal
2 = Slight

3 = Moderate
4 = Considerable
5 = Severe

When you apply this scoring system to the Stress Dynamics Scale, you will have a clearer picture of the degree of impact that each of the stressor's characteristics will have on you (refer to Chapter 2 for an explanation of each category):

_____ 1. Intensity (In)
_____ 2. Quality (Q)
_____ 3. Duration/Frequency (D/F)
_____ 4. Focus (F)
_____ 5. Extensity (E)
_____ 6. Mental/Physical Status (M/P)
_____ 7. Resistance (R)
_____ 8. Perception (P)

The individual scores provide you with valuable information about your stress. Those stress characteristics that rate higher will reflect the areas where you should focus your stress-management activities. For instance, if you were to rate a score of 4 points on the scale for Duration (D/F), and 5 points on Resistance (R), and 2 points on Focus (F), it would make sense for you to direct your energies toward working on increasing your resistance to the stressor, followed by reducing your duration of exposure to it. Because Focus (F) rated the lowest score, it would receive lower priority than the other two activities.

OTHER INDICATORS OF STRESS

Now that your awareness of your stress has increased, I suggest you once again review the table depicting the indications of stress (Table 1-1). Note which indications of stress you may currently be experiencing. After you have done this, refer to the Stress Dynamics Scale (Figure 3–4), page 50. Note the phases of flight where you experience the most stress.

Now look at the Nonfunctioning Stress Profile (NSP) and the Maximum Functioning Stress Profile (MFSP) in Chapter 2. Where would you rate yourself on each of these profiles?

Having assessed the various dimensions of your stress, it is now time to think about what you can do to reduce the stressors in your life. Take a moment and list on a piece of paper the immediate action steps you can take to accomplish this. After you have made your list, start taking action as soon as possible. The chapters that follow will provide you with tools and methods that I use regularly in my private practice to help pilots reduce and manage their stress. These chapters are also designed to provide you with the structure you will need to carry out effective stress-management activities.

10

Relaxation Techniques

Tension and relaxation are two sides of the same coin. They cannot exist at the same time. When the pilot is chronically tense, he must learn to relax. Otherwise he will experience greater levels of stress.

When I see a tense pilot walk into my office, I am fully aware of the fact that he is less flexible than he could be, both physically and mentally. Tension tends to limit the pilot's ability to act in ways that are not overly rigid. People who are calm tend to be more logical, practical, and confident. People who are tense tend to be more emotionally reactive to stressful situations. They tend to overfocus (channelize), take things more personally, and, in many cases, overreact. Confidence is often replaced by anxiety and worry. From observing the effects of tension on pilots, I have found that relaxation is a necessary step toward developing the "three C's" exhibited by pilots who manage stress effectively. These are:

CALMNESS
COMFORT
CONFIDENCE

A pilot who fully experiences these conditions feels better able to deal with his stressors.

Stress can cause the pilot to feel tense, uncomfortable, and incompetent. These feelings will usually become manifested in his personal and occupational life. This is because the pilot will fall into a trap that all humans fall into: we all tend to act out in our lives that person we believe ourselves to be. If we believe we are incompetent, we will usually behave incompetently. It is true that competence cannot come about without proper skill, knowledge, and ability. However, the pilot's negative beliefs, brought on by stress, can cause him to act incompetently. Of course, when the pilot is aware that he is not performing as well as he can, this could lead to more stress.

Pilots who experience high levels of stress often report that they know they are just not themselves. When I ask these pilots if they take time out to relax each day, nine times out of ten I receive the same response: "I don't have time." When I hear a pilot tell me this, I hear a deeper message, which is: "I have no control of my time or my life."

Stress management for the pilot means taking control. We cannot control our stress until we take control of our lives. Here are some of the reasons why some pilots do not have control of their time, hence their lives:

- Role overload
- Role ambiguity
- Poor planning
- Poor time-management
- Too many distractions
- Lack of commitment
- Lack of follow-through
- Lack of focus

- Procrastination
- Inability to say "no"
- The need to impress others
- Fear of rejection
- Fear of losing status among peers
- Fear of being expendable on the job
- Failure to delegate responsibility for tasks that others can accomplish

These are only a few of the problems that keep pilots from taking time to relax. We have all experienced periods in our lives in which most of these factors have influenced our behavior. I suggest that you pause for a moment and carefully reread the list. Be honest with yourself and note which of these are problem areas for you. Remember, you must become aware that a problem exists before you can solve it.

Once you take control of your time, you will find that many of the things you have been doing were inefficiently done. Time management is very important for the pilot who wants to live a less stressful life. Having more time available does not necessarily mean that you are lazy or unproductive. Let your accomplishments be the measure of your productivity. In many cases having free time equates to working smarter.

Of course, free time without relaxation does not make sense. I am now going to provide you with the opportunity to learn the relaxation exercises I have developed for pilots. They are simple to perform and can be mastered quickly. They are designed to help the pilot derive maximum benefit in a matter of minutes. When you first do these exercises, they will take from ten to fifteen minutes to complete. As you practice them and become more familiar with them, they will take less time.

There is one caution I will make for both of the exercises described in this chapter:

**DO NOT ATTEMPT ANY OF THESE RELAXA-
TION EXERCISES WHILE OPERATING AN AIR-
CRAFT, A MOTOR VEHICLE, OR ANY TYPE OF
MACHINERY.**

I also recommend that the pilot refrain from doing
these exercises for at least one hour prior to operating
any aircraft, motor vehicle, or other machinery. There
are a couple of reasons for this. First, relaxation may
make you drowsy. This is particularly true if you do the
exercise when tired. Second, when concentrating on the
relaxation exercise, your attention will be diverted from
other important things. If, for instance, while flying, you
were to engage in the practice of a relaxation exercise,
you might miss a radio call from ATC or an indication
that you have crossed a navigation fix. Worse yet, you
might not spot critical traffic and wind up in a midair
collision.

Be careful. *Do these exercises while you are on the
ground.* With regular use, the positive benefits should be
felt both on the ground and in flight. I have taught these
techniques to many pilots and have had excellent results.
Follow the instructions carefully. They will help you to
master the exercises quickly and easily.

THE PILOT STRESS RELAXATION EXERCISE

The first relaxation technique I will introduce you to can
be used to relax your body, while instilling physical and
emotional calmness. I recommend doing this exercise
twice a day. Some pilots prefer to do it once in the
morning and then again in the evening, before sleep.
Others use it prior to going into highly stressful situations.

There are two ways this exercise can be done. The first

method, which I refer to as the *directed method,* incorporates the use of second-person statements beginning with the words "you" or "your." For example, while doing this exercise you may say to yourself, "You are now allowing the muscles in your upper arms to relax." This approach is "directed" because the phrases used while doing the exercise will be similar to those that one person would tell another to direct them to do something.

The second approach, the *"self-directed" approach,* is self-explanatory. Phrases such as "I am releasing the tension in my upper arms" and "I am feeling more calm and more comfortable" will be used.

Your task will be to choose one of these two approaches. Your selection should be based on your own preference. If you tend to prefer guidance from others when beginning new tasks, you may prefer the directed approach. If you are a natural do-it-yourselfer, the self-directed approach might be in order. Neither approach is more effective than the other. Some pilots respond more readily to direction from others, while others are more comfortable directing themselves.

I will present a script for each approach. You do not have to follow the script exactly as it is presented. You may change some of the words or phrases to meet your own needs. Some pilots prefer to memorize the script. This is okay too. It is important that you understand each task to be accomplished and that you accomplish them in their proper order. If you prefer, you may use a tape recorder to record the scripts. The tape can then be played back while doing the exercises. Taped scripts make good learning tools. Some pilots prefer to have the exercise on tape, while others prefer to verbalize the script to themselves without the use of a tape. You may wish to use a tape until you have become thoroughly familiar with the exercise, then discard the tape. This is up to you.

The Pilot Stress Relaxation Exercise consists of six important steps. Each step must be completed in order to benefit from this exercise. These steps are as follows:

1. Sit in a comfortable position. I do not recommend doing this exercise while lying down unless you wish to fall asleep.
2. Take three deep breaths. As you do this, slowly inhale while thinking of the word "calmness," and imagine yourself exhaling "tension." The simple act of taking the deep breaths will initiate the relaxation process.
3. Close your eyes and relax every muscle in your body while saying the words "calmness and comfort." As you do this you will be associating calmness and comfort with relaxation. In time this association will become very strong and you will be able to create calmness and comfort in your body by merely saying the words "calmness and comfort" silently to yourself.
4. Scan your body for any indication of tension. When tension is found, focus your concentration on the tense muscle and imagine calmness and comfort entering it. This should be done while allowing yourself to release the tension. If you find it difficult to release a tense muscle, you can exaggerate the tension on that muscle, hold that tension for a few seconds, and release the tension while thinking the words "calmness and comfort."
5. Once the muscles are all calm and relaxed, keep scanning your body while saying the words "calmness and comfort" to yourself. Do this for a few minutes so that you will be sure to remove all tension from your body.
6. When you are ready to end the exercise, place your feet flat on the floor and feel them making contact with

the ground. This is very important because when pilots are stressed they tend to lack a firm, grounded, stable feeling. By physically feeling your feet making contact with the ground, you will feel more firmly planted. Once this feeling is experienced, open your eyes.

When doing the Pilot Stress Relaxation Exercise, you will be accomplishing the six steps listed above. Each of these tasks is incorporated into the scripts that follow. Do the exercise slowly and space out each phrase and each sentence so that you can give your body time to relax.

DIRECTED SCRIPT

Sit in a comfortable position. . . . Now take three deep breaths . . . inhaling calmness . . . and exhaling tension . . . deeply and slowly . . . calmly and comfortably. . . . As you continue to do this, draw your attention to the tips of your toes. . . . Now imagine calmness entering your feet . . . moving from the tips of your toes . . . down through your feet . . . into your heels . . . feeling very calm . . . very comfortable . . . and very relaxed. . . . Now imagine the calmness and comfort spreading into your ankles . . . and continuing to spread into the muscles of your calves . . . releasing tension . . . and replacing tension with more calmness and comfort. . . . And the calmness and comfort continue to spread into your knees . . . and into your thighs . . . calmly and comfortably releasing tension . . . and allowing the muscles in your thighs . . . to become more calm . . . and more relaxed. . . . As the calmness continues to spread into your hips . . . and all of the muscles around your hips . . . allow the calmness and comfort to spread into your buttocks muscles . . . releasing tension . . . and replacing tension with relaxation. . . . And the calmness and comfort continue to spread into your stomach muscles . . . allowing them to grow loose and limp . . . just releasing tension . . . and allowing calmness and comfort to replace the tension. . . . Now the calmness and comfort continue to spread into your lower back . . . and slowly move into your upper back . . . allowing the muscles in your upper back to grow loose and limp. . . . And imagine the calmness and comfort spreading into your chest as you notice your breathing . . . very slow . . . and very rhythmic . . . calmly and comfortably . . . inhaling calmness . . . and exhaling tension. . . . And the calmness and comfort continue to spread into your shoulders . . . releasing pent-up tension . . . and pent-up responsibilities. . . . As the calmness and comfort now continue to spread down into your upper arms . . . your lower arms . . . your wrists . . . your hands . . . and your fingers. . . . Now draw your attention to your neck muscles . . . and imagine the calmness and comfort spreading from the front of your neck . . . slowly around into the back of your neck . . . releasing tension . . . and replacing tension with more calmness and comfort. . . . And the calmness and comfort continue to spread into the back of your scalp . . . up into the top of your scalp . . . and down over your eyelids . . . your facial muscles . . . and your jaws. . . . Now take a moment and once again concentrate on your breathing. . . . As you slowly inhale more calmness . . . and exhale tension. . . . Deeply and slowly . . . calmly and comfortably. . . . And now scan your body. . . . If you notice any tension . . . just focus on the spot where the tension is and allow the tension to release itself. . . . If you need to tighten the muscle where the tension is, tighten it for a few seconds . . . then release it . . . replacing tension with calmness and comfort. . . . You can continue to do this as long as you feel tension in your body . . . continuing to release tension . . . and replace that tension with calmness and comfort. . . . And when you are ready to

stop the exercise . . . just place your feet flat on the floor
. . . and feel your feet making contact with the ground
. . . and feel yourself firmly planted . . . and once you feel
firmly planted you may open your eyes.

SELF-DIRECTED SCRIPT

*(Sitting in a comfortable position with eyes closed, you may
say this to yourself out loud or quietly):* I am drawing my
attention to the tips of my toes. . . . I am now imagining
calmness and comfort . . . moving from the tips of my
toes . . . down through my feet into my heels. . . . And
the calmness and comfort is moving from my heels into
my ankles . . . and into my calves. . . . All of the muscles
of my calves are relaxing completely . . . releasing tension. . . . And the calmness continues to spread into my
knees . . . and into my thighs . . . releasing tension
. . . and replacing tension with more calmness and comfort. . . . Now the calmness and comfort continue to
spread into my hips . . . and all of the muscles and fibers
around my hips . . . releasing tension and replacing tension with comfort and relaxation. . . . As I release the
tension in the buttocks muscles . . . I continue to feel
more calm and more comfortable. . . . Now the calmness
and comfort moves into my stomach muscles . . . as I
allow them to become loose and limp . . . releasing tension and growing more calm and more comfortable.
. . . And the calmness and comfort continue to move into
my lower back . . . slowly spreading into my upper back
. . . calmly and comfortably releasing tension . . . as each
and every muscle in my upper back relaxes completely.
. . . And the calmness now moves into my chest . . . as
I breathe deeply and slowly . . . calmly and comfortably.
. . . Inhaling calmness . . . and exhaling tension . . . slowly
and rhythmically . . . calmly and comfortably. . . . Now
the calmness and comfort move into my shoulders . . . as

I release pent-up tension . . . and any pent-up responsibilities . . . and the calmness and comfort continue to
move down into my upper arms . . . my lower arms
. . . my wrists . . . my hands . . . and my fingers. . . . I
am now drawing my attention to my neck muscles . . .
allowing calmness and comfort to move from the front
of my neck . . . slowly around into the back of my neck.
. . . And the calmness and comfort move into the back
of my scalp . . . over the top of my scalp . . . and down
over my forehead . . . my eyelids . . . my facial muscles
. . . and my jaw. . . . I am now scanning my body to see
if I can feel any tension. . . . [*If you find a tense spot, say:
Here is a tense spot. . . . I will allow the tension to drift away
. . . as I allow calmness and comfort to enter my body.
. . . I will now allow my entire body to continue to
relax. . . .*] [*At this time continue to scan your body for any
signs of tension and repeat the relaxation as often as is
necessary to release the tension*]. . . . I will now concentrate
on my breathing . . . as I inhale calmness . . . and exhale
tension . . . calmly and comfortably . . . slowly and
rhythmically. . . . [*When you are ready to end the exercise,
say to yourself*]: I am now ready to end the exercise.
. . . I am placing my feet firmly on the floor . . . and I'm
feeling my feet firmly and solidly planted on the ground.
(*Now open your eyes.*)

THE LAYOVER SLEEP-RELAXATION
EXERCISE

Many pilots have complained that they have difficulty
falling asleep during their layover period. When they
finally do so, many have difficulty remaining asleep. In
Chapter 5 I addressed the issue of sleep problems.
Whether the sleep disturbance you are experiencing is
caused by jet lag or some other cause such as discomfort

with a new sleep environment, you can use this exercise to help you sleep better. The exercise is not designed to replace lost sleep due to a physical problem, so I highly recommend that if you continue to have sleep disturbance, or if it worsens after using this exercise, discontinue using the exercise and consult your AME.

This exercise, like the Pilot Stress Relaxation Exercise, can also be accomplished using the directed or self-directed approach. Again, select the approach with which you feel most comfortable. The steps for the Layover Sleep Relaxation Exercise are as follows:

1. Lie down. Make sure that you are comfortable and that the lights in the room are out.
2. Close your eyes and take three deep breaths. This will help you relax. Imagine yourself inhaling calmness and exhaling tension.
3. Relax every muscle in your body while saying the words "calmness and comfort."
4. Scan your body for any indication of tension. When tension is found, focus your concentration on the tense muscle and say the words "calmness and comfort." As in the Pilot Stress Relaxation Exercise, you can tighten any tense muscle and hold the tension for a few seconds and then release it. Remember to repeat the words "calmness and comfort" as you do this.
5. When your body is thoroughly relaxed, use the imagery that is presented in the script.

Don't become discouraged if when you first try this exercise you do not fall asleep right away, for with time and practice you should be able to obtain positive results. I suggest you practice this exercise while at home. You will become familiar with it quicker than if you practice only while on layovers. An added benefit of home practice is success in a familiar environment. By easily achieving sleep through the use of this exercise while at home, you should be able to take the same exercise with you to your layover destination and make it work there.

As you review the script for the Layover Sleep Relaxation Exercise, you may notice a close similarity to the Pilot Stress Relaxation Exercise scripts. While the two exercises are similar in many respects, they are fundamentally different. The Pilot Stress Relaxation Exercise is oriented toward reduction of stress through tension reduction. The Layover Sleep Relaxation Exercise, on the other hand, is geared toward the specific purpose of sleep. Specific words are used in this exercise to guide you through a process called "imagery."

Some people find it difficult to visualize objects or events in their mind's eye. If you are one of these people, don't worry about visualizing. Just imagine (think about) what you are telling yourself while following the script. It is not necessary for you to possess the ability to visualize while doing the exercise. Again, a tape recorder may be useful.

THE LAYOVER SLEEP RELAXATION EXERCISE SCRIPT

Close your eyes and take three deep breaths . . . inhaling calmness . . . and exhaling tension . . . deeply and slowly . . . calmly and comfortably. . . . As you continue to do this draw your attention to the tips of your toes. . . . Now imagine calmness entering your feet . . . moving from the tips of your toes . . . down through your feet . . . into your heels . . . feeling very calm . . . very comfortable . . . and very relaxed. . . . Now imagine the calmness and comfort spreading into your ankles . . . and continuing to spread into the muscles of your calves . . . releasing tension

. . . and replacing tension with more calmness and comfort. . . . And the calmness and comfort continues to
spread into your knees . . . and into your thighs . . . calmly
and comfortably releasing tension . . . and allowing the
muscles in your thighs . . . to become more calm . . . and
more relaxed. . . . As the calmness continues to spread
into your hips . . . and all of the muscles around your hips
. . . allow the calmness and comfort to spread into your
buttocks muscles . . . releasing tension . . . and replacing
tension with relaxation. . . . And the calmness and comfort continue to spread into your stomach muscles . . .
allowing them to grow loose and limp . . . just releasing
tension . . . and allowing calmness and comfort to replace
the tension. . . . Now the calmness and comfort continue
to spread into your lower back . . . and slowly move into
your upper back . . . allowing the muscles in your upper
back to grow loose and limp. . . . And imagine the calmness and comfort spreading into your chest as you notice
your breathing . . . very slow . . . and very rhythmic.
. . . Calmly and comfortably . . . inhaling calmness
. . . and exhaling tension. . . . And the calmness and
comfort continue to spread into your shoulders . . .
releasing pent-up tension . . . and pent-up responsibilities. . . . As the calmness and comfort now continue to
spread down into your upper arms . . . your lower arms
. . . your wrists . . . your hands . . . and your fingers.
. . . Now draw your attention to your neck muscles
. . . and imagine calmness and comfort spreading from
the front of your neck . . . slowly around into the back
of your neck . . . releasing tension . . . and replacing
tension with more calmness and comfort. . . . And the
calmness and comfort continue to spread into the back
of your scalp . . . up into the top of your scalp . . . and
down over your eyelids . . . your facial muscles . . . and
your jaws. . . . Now take a moment and once again
concentrate on your breathing. . . . As you slowly inhale

more calmness . . . and exhale tension. . . . Deeply and
slowly . . . calmly and comfortably. . . . And now scan
your body. . . . If you notice any tension . . . just focus
on the spot where the tension is and allow the tension to
release itself. . . . If you need to tighten the muscle where
the tension is, tighten it for a few seconds . . . then release
it . . . replacing tension with calmness and comfort
. . . continuing to release tension . . . and allowing calmness and comfort to enter. . . . And just become aware
of your relaxation . . . as you now imagine yourself in a
very calm and relaxing place. . . . It can be on a beach
. . . or a mountain . . . in a special room . . . or anyplace
you want it to be. . . . This is your place . . . a place where
you are free of tension and anxiety. . . . It's a place where
you can relax . . . and be free of the stressors in your life.
. . . As you become aware of this special place . . . imagine
yourself looking around you. . . . What's in your environment? . . . Are you alone or are you with another person
or other people? . . . Notice what you're wearing . . . and
what you're doing. . . . As you observe yourself in your
special place . . . imagine yourself remaining calm . . .
comfortable . . . and relaxed. . . . Feeling very positive.
. . . Feeling comfortable. . . . And imagine that you are
looking at a simple object in your environment . . . an
object that reminds you of something that is calm and
soothing. . . . The object can be something that is a part
of nature . . . such as the setting sun. . . . Or it can be
manmade . . . such as a boat. . . . Notice the color or
colors of the object. . . . How many colors can you see?
. . . Is the object large or small? . . . Notice the qualities
of the object that remind you of calmness, comfort, and
relaxation. . . . Now imagine yourself continuing to release more tension. . . . As you feel yourself in that
relaxing environment . . . feel the air touching your body
. . . feeing pleasant. . . . Not too warm. . . . Not too cool.
. . . Just right. . . . And take a moment to feel the calm

and comfortable temperature. . . . And now imagine yourself touching something in the environment. . . . Something that feels relaxing to you . . . something that feels comfortable. . . . And pay attention to the sounds in this calm and relaxing environment. . . . What do they sound like? . . . Listen for calm rhythm . . . as you listen very comfortably. . . . And imagine yourself smelling something that is very pleasant . . . a smell that reminds you of this calm and relaxing place. . . . Notice if it reminds you of a memory from the past that was pleasant. . . . Maybe you can even taste the calm and relaxing fragrance . . . a very pleasant and relaxing taste . . . and you may continue to explore your calm and comfortable environment. . . . And as you do this . . . notice your breathing . . . calm and comfortable . . . slow and rhythmic. . . . As you continue to release tension . . . and relax completely. [Continue the exercise as long as you wish.]

In the Layover Sleep Relaxation Exercise I introduce a guided imagery approach that pilots find very calming. You can use as your special calm place any type of environment you choose. It can be a warm, tropical beach, the deck of a boat, a mountaintop, or a room filled with objects you associate with calmness and relaxation. You can be as creative as you like. The place you choose is a private place. You can have anybody in it you wish. Or you may prefer to be alone.

The imagery you use may be different from the script I have provided. Some pilots feel more calm when they are actively doing something. Some prefer to remain passive while watching others engage in restful activities such as windsurfing or kite flying.

Continue the exercise until you fall asleep. At first it may take time, but as you become more familiar with your private place, you will find yourself more easily drifting off to restful sleep.

Again, this exercise can be accomplished through the directed and self-directed approaches—I have presented the directed version. Should you choose to use the self-directed approach, just modify the script to reflect self-directed statements. The self-directed script for the Pilot Stress Relaxation Exercise can be used as a guide to help you develop your own self-directed script for this exercise.

CONDITIONING RELAXATION

When behavior is rewarded it tends to be repeated. Positive rewards condition us to behave in ways that will bring about additional rewards. The reward is the payoff. Calmness and comfort in the presence of major stressors have several payoffs for the pilot. These include:

- Less anxiety
- Feeling of competence to meet the demands of stressors
- Feeling of being in control
- Ability to think calmly and soundly
- Less distraction
- Ability to avoid channelizing
- Increased ability to function in one's role as a pilot
- Increased ability to solve problems
- Channels of communication remain open
- Ability to avoid role overload
- Lower incidence of occupational burnout
- Increased confidence
- Better physical health
- Positive mental attitude
- Increased flexibility
- Increased resourcefulness

By regularly doing the Pilot Stress Relaxation and Layover Sleep Relaxation Exercises you will be conditioning yourself to maintain the benefits listed above.

There are a couple of techniques I have found to be useful in facilitating the conditioning process. I would like to share them with you.

The first technique is the finger squeeze. This seems very simple but its effects can be powerful. I have my clients use it anytime they are in a situation they find to be extremely stressful. I tell them that when they feel stress coming on, all they have to do is squeeze the thumb and second finger of one hand together. I usually recommend using the left hand because this hand stimulates right-brain activity. The right side of the brain controls the left side of the body. It is also where the emotional aspects of one's personality exist.

However, calmness and comfort cannot just come about simply by squeezing the thumb and second finger of your left hand together. These emotions must first become conditioned (or learned). The conditioning process is simple. All you have to do is squeeze the thumb and second finger of your left hand together when doing the Pilot Stress Relaxation Exercise. With your thumb and finger squeezed, and your body relaxed, repeat the words "calmness and comfort" several times. Do this every time you do the exercise. Keep in mind that you do not have to do the finger squeeze during the entire relaxation exercise to develop this conditioning. In time you should be able to merely do the finger squeeze and experience immediate calmness and comfort, wherever you are.

Another technique I teach pilots is similar but is applied in a different manner. This is the hand-press technique. When you wish to experience calmness and comfort rapidly, all you have to do is press on the back of your left hand with the first two fingers of your right hand. Once again, this stimulates right-brain activity and is initially conditioned in the same manner as the finger squeeze technique.

There are several advantages and disadvantages to each of these techniques. The finger squeeze has on its plus side its ready availability to the pilot, regardless of his location; its effectiveness in use for rapid creation of calmness and comfort for the pilot; and its lack of obviousness while being applied. It can also be used while doing other tasks, as only the thumb and second finger of one hand are used. The disadvantage of this technique is that it is not as effective as the hand press. Most pilots who use the hand press report that its effects are more pronounced. I do not know why this is so, but I would hypothesize it is because a larger area of the hand (and thus the right brain) is stimulated.

Other positive advantages of the hand press include its effectiveness in rapidly creating calmness and comfort for the pilot, and the longer-lasting effects that come from the lingering sensation that is felt after the hand has been pressed. This causes the pilot to continue to associate the feeling of calmness and comfort long after he has discontinued the hand press. There are two major disadvantages of this technique. First, it cannot be used unless both hands are free, and second, it is very obvious. It cannot be used inconspicuously among a group of people (unless everybody in the group has read this book and is so familiar with the technique that they think nothing of it when someone uses it). Again, I do not recommend using either of these techniques while operating aircraft, motor vehicles, or machinery.

RELAXATION INSIDE THE COCKPIT

Flying can become very tense and stressful for the pilot. Mastery of the exercises and techniques presented thus far should be of great help in reducing your overall stress and tension levels. But there will be those times when you will need exercises you can use for relaxation in the cockpit—exercises that won't interfere with normal flight operation and duties. I have found that short, simple relaxation exercises seem to work best.

Breathing Exercises

When we are tense we tend to breathe in a somewhat rapid, constricted fashion. This exercise will help you slow down and normalize your breathing.

First, take a deep breath. Hold it for a few seconds, then release it. Repeat this three times. Be careful not to move too quickly through this exercise. Now consciously slow down your breathing and try to establish a more comfortable rhythm.

Shoulder Raise-Drop

Raise your shoulders as high as you can. Hold your shoulders in this position for 3 to 5 seconds. Now drop them. Repeat this exercise until your shoulders release tension.

Head Rotation

Tilt your head forward and slowly rotate it clockwise. Once you have made a full circle, rotate it in the other direction. Repeat this three times in each direction. If you find yourself getting dizzy, slow down—you're moving too fast.

Muscle Tense-Release

Tighten then release the major muscles of the body. Be sure to include your fists, arms, and facial muscles.

Self-Massage

Massaging the muscles of your face, scalp, neck, shoulders, and arms can be very relaxing.

11

Problem Solving

Problems are not new to the pilot. They are encountered from the first time he enters the cockpit during his primary flight training and they continue to be experienced throughout his professional career.

The nature of problems varies for the pilot. They can be job-related or they can originate in his personal life.

The stress a problem creates can be great, especially if the problem is one that could have extremely negative consequences. Problems that are most stressful to pilots are (1) those that are life threatening, (2) those that threaten his own or a loved one's status or security (occupational, marital, or economic), and (3) those that are persistent or recurring. Numbers 2 and 3 can impose an annoyance that can be stressful even if the problem is a minor one.

Some problems are much more difficult to solve than others. But regardless of the nature or difficulty of the pilot's problems, the basic strategies he uses to solve them can be simple and easy to learn. One such strategy will be examined in this chapter, but first it will be helpful to understand why problems occur in the first place.

THE NATURE OF PROBLEMS

A problem exists when there is a desire or need to find a method to make one or more objects, events, or situations fit, take place, or work out. Using this definition, we can see that problems are not necessarily caused by errors or breakdowns that occur when something ceases to work properly or smoothly. This is particularly true when an object, event, or situation must be matched with another object, event, or situation. For instance, a problem exists when a pilot, experienced in flying one type of aircraft, is to be assigned to another type of aircraft. Here the pilot (object) must be matched with a new aircraft (situation). If the match does not fit, a dangerous situation will exist. The problem, then, would be to find a way to make the match work out. The solution would be thorough training.

There are a number of sources of problems of which all pilots should be aware. Some of these are within his control, while others are not. Existing outside the pilot's control are some problems related to aircraft design flaws and faulty maintenance. These conditions might not become known to the pilot until an emergency situation arises. Unforeseeable events can also be due to causes beyond the pilot's control.

Within the scope of the pilot's control are a number of problem causes. These include mental overload; poor management of available resources; lack of knowledge, training, or experience; illness; poor planning; and in some cases, perceptual limitations.

We have already examined mental overload in Chapter 3. It can occur whenever the pilot is very busy or has too much on his mind. But it tends to increase more rapidly when stress is present in the pilot's life.

Poor management of available resources continues to be a major cause of problems that exist at all levels of aviation. In the cockpit, resources can be divided into five categories: human resources, equipment, information, consumables, and procedures.

• Human resources include the crew, air traffic controllers, flight service personnel, and others who can contribute to problem solving by providing information or other forms of assistance.

• Equipment resources include the aircraft controls and instrument (and placard) displays, and any objects or tools that can be used to enhance problem solving.

• Information is a resource that may be presented to the pilot through conscious thought, or sensory input (sight, hearing, touch, smell, or taste). Typical sources of information available to the pilot are his knowledge and experience, of which he may be consciously and intuitively aware; observations of instrument and other avionics displays, traffic, geographical markers, etc.; printed material, such as charts, weather reports, computer printouts, the Airman's Information Manual, the flight operations manual, etc.; verbal messages from other crewmembers, air traffic controllers, the pilots of other aircraft, transmitted ATIS, NOTAM, and PIREP information, the company frequency, etc.

• Consumable resources are those that will become less available or be depleted as time progresses. These resources must be monitored carefully because once they are spent they will no longer be available during a particular flight. They include items such as fuel and oil, time, duty time, and pilot alertness.

• Procedures represent the final category. They help the pilot fly the aircraft in a manner that ensures safety and efficiency.

Lack of knowledge, training, or experience can be

problem causes over which pilots have control. When a deficit is discovered, the pilot should take steps to gain as much knowledge, training, or experience as possible to close the gap. Stress can dramatically interfere with the pilot's ability to operate as he normally would. Knowledge gained through training and experience tends to increase the pilot's ability to withstand the negative effects of stress.

Illness can lead to a number of problems. It can cause distraction through discomfort, decreased ability to remember and think clearly, and it can slow the pilot's physical reaction time. Awareness of the presence of illness is important for the pilot. He must recognize that if he is ill he may not operate as he normally would; and problems might develop.

Poor planning usually occurs when pilots are pressed for time, are complacent, or have received inadequate (incomplete or ambiguous) information. The pilot must be aware of the possibility that one or more of these conditions can exist at any time. All can cause problems.

As humans, we all have perceptual limitations. These were noted in Chapter 3 (see Figures 3-1 and 3-2). By erroneously filling in the informational gaps that exist, problems may develop. This is particularly true when the information made available to the pilot is inadequate or wrong. Awareness of these perceptual limitations can help the pilot to double check his information to ensure that he is not operating on a false premise. This will help reduce problems caused by the pilot's perceptual limitations.

SOLVING PROBLEMS

When problems are recognized, the following seven steps can be taken to solve them:

1. Define the problem.
2. Evaluate the resources that are available to solve the problem.
3. Examine possible solutions.
4. Choose the best solution.
5. Implement the chosen solution by taking action.
6. Monitor and evaluate the results.
7. Make corrections as necessary.

Define the Problem

Before any problem can be solved, it must first be defined. What is the problem? The pilot may be aware that a problem exists because he does not know how he will accomplish a task; or he may realize something he has done isn't working out as he had planned. At times a problem's definition may be obvious, as in the case of an illuminated warning light in the cockpit. In many cases, however, definition isn't so simple. When this happens, the pilot must draw upon his available resources to help him. These resources could include instrument display readings, other crewmembers, or the flight manual.

In defining the problem, the pilot must ask himself which object or objects, events, or situations are involved. Then he must determine whether it (or they) must be fitted, take place, or work out. Once this has been done, the pilot will be more aware of his starting point (the problem) and his goal (the desired outcome). This approach can work with many different types of problems the pilot may encounter. A client, whom I will call Jim, had a problem he had to define.

Jim, a thirty-year-old first officer, was experiencing a great degree of stress. It was related to a demanding schedule he had voluntarily taken on. At first the schedule didn't appear to create problems for him, but after a short period of time he began to notice his wife and children were not comfortable with his extended periods of being away from home. Jim liked his schedule but knew it was creating problems in his marriage and in the family. He also knew that if he didn't continue to fly the particular run he was on, he might have to take a pay cut that would put financial stress on his family.

I started working with Jim and we began defining the problem. First, I had him list the objects, events, or situations involved:

OBJECT   = _____
EVENT   = _____
SITUATION   = Schedule takes me away from home too much

Next I had him determine whether something had to fit, take place, or work out. He thought about this and then made the following list:

FIT   = Schedule to meet my needs and my family's needs

TAKE PLACE   =

WORK OUT   = Be able to meet my own needs and the needs of my family without receiving a cut in pay

Jim was then instructed to join the completed items from both lists:

SITUATION   = Schedule takes me away from home too much

FIT   = Schedule to meet my needs and my family's needs

WORK OUT   = Be able to meet my own needs (not receive pay cut) and the needs of my family (be home more)

Once this was accomplished, Jim was able to see that his problem involved a situation that had to fit with something in order to work out in a way that would allow him to have his own needs met as well as meeting the needs of his family. He was then able to define his problem succinctly:

> My problem is that I have to find a way to have a schedule that will allow me to maintain the same level of pay that I am currently receiving, while spending more time with my family.

This definition gave Jim a clear picture of what his problem was and where he wanted his solution to take him.

Jim's problem was more simple to define than many you may encounter in your personal and professional life. But the steps taken will be the same. By breaking the problem down into a *simple problem statement,* you will find yourself much less overwhelmed and confused.

Of course there will be times when you will be unable to take the time to go through the steps presented here. This is especially true in cockpit emergency situations. In such cases, when procedures are available, follow them. Whether procedures are available or not, don't hesitate to ask for assistance from others to help you determine the source of your problem.

Evaluate the Resources Available to Solve the Problem

The second step in the problem-solving process requires awareness of the available resources that can be of help in solving the problem. Other crewmembers, flight service and ATC personnel, information from various sources, and the company frequency are some of the many resources available to the pilot.

During this stage of problem solving you should consider your resources as tools. Lay them out on the table by listing them and discussing them with others involved in the problem-solving process.

Jim listed his resources:

1. Chief pilot
2. Dispatcher
3. Pilots with more experience
   A. Don
   B. Erika
   C. Alan

After making his list, Jim considered with which of these people he should discuss the problem. He opted to talk first to Alan, a pilot who had been flying with the airline six years longer than Jim; he would then talk to the dispatcher. He didn't want to talk to the chief pilot until he had more information.

Examine the Possible Solutions

Once you have evaluated your resources, look at the various ways in which you can use them to come up with a number of possible solutions. Then list the pros and cons of each.

Jim spoke with Alan and the dispatcher. From his conversations he was able to come up with four possible solutions:

> 1. Bid for a run that will originate from the Midwest. It will allow me to maintain my current level of pay and spend much more time with my family.
>
> *Pros*
> A. It will be cheaper for us to live in the Midwest.
> B. We will be getting away from the crowded city.

Cons

A. I will have to pack the family up and move. This may be a hassle.

B. We will be leaving all of our friends and family behind.

C. I will have to contend with flight in bad weather.

2. Remain on the current run for three more months. At that time better runs will open up for bid.

Pros

A. My wife and family will know that I will be spending more time with them in three months. This should ease up the pressures and bring down my stress level.

B. I will be able to maintain my current level of pay, allowing us to live a better life-style.

C. I'll be able to enjoy flying more because the family will be off my back.

Cons

A. My wife and family might not feel better about this solution, and things might worsen at home.

B. I may continue to experience stress.

C. I might be passing up a good thing by not moving to the Midwest. They say things are going to go real well there.

3. Leave this run now and bid for one that will provide me with more time to spend with my family. Then bid for a higher-paying run in three months when the better runs open up.

Pros

A. My family will enjoy having me around more.

B. I'll feel less pressure from the family.

C. I'll be more rested.

Cons

A. Less money. That will mean tightening the purse strings for at least three months.

B. The cut in pay may create more pressure in the family.
C. I might be missing my chance in the Midwest.

4. Try any of the previous solutions, and if things don't work out, return to my present run.

Pros

A. I won't be financially worse off if I have to do this.
B. Things will be getting better later on this year. More bids will open up.

Cons

A. I may be stuck in the same rut if I have to use this option.
B. It may cause a lot of stress for me and my family if I have to return to this run.
C. I may feel like I've failed my family.
D. My family may feel like I've failed them.

Choose the Best Solution

Choosing the best solution to a problem can be difficult at times, especially when the consequences of choosing the wrong solution can have disastrous results. Careful analysis of each of the possible solutions, along with their pros and cons, is necessary before the best solution can be chosen. In this analysis, the pilot should ask himself all the possible "what if's" that can occur in each selection choice. These should then, if at all possible, be discussed with those who are directly involved with solving the problem. At times it may be of benefit to bring in an objective third party to provide feedback.

Jim carefully examined his options. He did this first while alone, then with his wife and children. Each family member was presented with the pros and cons, and each was provided with an opportunity to communicate his or her feelings about the solutions. In a short period of time, Jim and his wife chose Jim's first solution. Jim and his family were thrilled at the thought of relocating to the Midwest. The family saw it as an adventure. Jim realized that his financial and occupational needs would be met, while his family would be able to enjoy his presence in the household.

Implement the Chosen Solution by Taking Action

Once the solution has been chosen, it must be applied to the problem. This is the only way we can know whether it will work. Sometimes other solutions will become known during this stage of problem solving. This can occur by accident. Think of all the times in your life when you made an attempt to solve a problem by using one solution, only to wind up discovering a more effective one. Problems with implementing the solution may also be encountered during this stage. But more often than not, problems of this kind become learning tools that will help you become a more sophisticated problem solver.

Jim discovered that his move to the Midwest would not be as easy as he had at first thought. He was able to obtain reassignment to the new location, but he had difficulties with the moving company. There were delays, and furniture had been damaged. For the first month in his new domicile, Jim also had to make some major adjustments. Though he was still working for the same airline, he felt as if he were working in another world. Everybody seemed to be moving at a much slower pace than he had been used to.

Monitor the Results

There comes a time in every problem-solving endeavor when all that can be done has been done. At this time, the pilot is left with the task of watching to see what result the solution will bring about. In time, feedback will come. This will let the pilot know whether his chosen and implemented solution was a valid one.

Jim wasn't sure of the effects of his solution until he had been at his new domicile for two months. He had made some new friends, and his family had settled into its new home. At first Jim wasn't sure that he liked the slower pace of life in the new city, but he adjusted to it rapidly.

Make Corrections as Necessary

If your solution does not turn out to be the best one, you may have to make corrections. In many cases the corrections required will be minor. At times, however, major corrections may become necessary to remedy a faulty solution. When this is the case the original problem—or the resulting problem—may have to be reworked. If this becomes necessary, it is often helpful to reanalyze each step of your problem-solving approach. Pay particular attention to your original problem definition and the resources you had available to you, versus those that you used and the various solutions that you came up with. Also, the manner in which you implemented your solution (even if it was a viable one) could have had a negative effect on the outcome of the problem.

The problem-solving strategy presented here is one that you can use in your personal and professional life, but there are two cautions you should bear in mind:

First, don't attempt to use this approach in an emergency situation requiring immediate action. In such cases it is often far more effective to rely on your own skill, training, and experience. Procedures you have learned and practiced are called for here. But nothing replaces sound, rational thinking in an emergency.

Second, if a problem seems to be getting out of hand, don't hesitate for a moment to obtain assistance from others. I know that this should go without saying, but it can't be stressed enough—I have read too many aircraft accident reports to feel otherwise.

Problem solving is an integral part of stress management for the pilot. Regular use of this approach can help reduce the stress that creates further problems in your life.

If you're wondering what ever became of Jim, we last spoke a few months ago, which was two years after he left the Los Angeles area. He is now a captain for his airline and has told me he feels the solution he and his family chose was, indeed, the best possible.

12

Interacting with Yourself and Others

The things that we and others tell us about our stressors can serve to reduce, maintain, or increase our stress. Hence, how we interact with ourselves and others is an important consideration in the management of pilot stress.

INTERACTING WITH YOURSELF

Self-Criticalness

When stress is experienced, the pilot's self-criticalness usually increases. Unfortunately, so does his vulnerability to the negative effects that self-criticalness can have on his self-esteem and the performance of his duties.

If you are one of those pilots who tends to become overly self-critical when things aren't going well, you must become aware of the potential dangers involved.

The first of these is that the effects of self-criticalness become intensified when stress is present.

The second danger involves the mental block to problem solving that can arise. The self-critical pilot may feel that he doesn't have what it takes to solve the problem and then becomes ineffective at solving the problem.

The third danger involves the tendency of the self-critical pilot to become overly focused on his inadequacies and inabilities, while ignoring his more functional traits and abilities. This serves to create a blindness to the personal resources, that can be used to solve his problems. These resources include his ability to analyze and assess the problem situation, and his knowledge, skills, and experience.

The fourth danger lies in the pilot's tendency to stop listening to others who may try to provide support. This often comes from the tendency of the self-critical pilot not to hear anything which others will say that contradicts the self-critical image he holds of himself.

All of these dangers add up to a pilot whose ability to solve problems is impaired. Proper use of the stress-management approaches presented in this book will help reduce the stress that intensifies self-criticalness, but you must work toward reducing the criticalness that you hold toward yourself.

Be careful not to confuse self-criticalness with self-discipline. Self-criticalness involves self-punishment and degradation. Self-discipline involves acknowledgment of one's potentials and abilities and the willingness to put them to use.

People who are overly self-critical must first learn that it is okay to make mistakes. We all learn by making them. They must also learn to acknowledge and emphasize their strengths. When I see a person who is overly self-critical I immediately think of the word "rigid." That is because self-criticalness reflects a quality of inflexibility toward those things that make us human—things like saying and doing the wrong things at times. If you are a rigid person, work at loosening up a little. Find a friend or colleague who can help you do this. It will help you develop a little more flexibility that can be used to deal with the stressors in your life.

Who Am I?

Though it is true that more pilots are acknowledging their thoughts and feelings, I am finding that many still are not. These pilots support the old personality profile of the pilot being a nonintrospective individual. If you are one of these pilots and you are serious about managing pilot stress, now is the time to stop supporting the outdated nonintrospective stereotype.

Refusal to look at oneself often reflects a fear of discovering something about oneself that won't be comfortable. I feel that denial of those aspects of one's personality or psychological makeup does not allow the individual to improve those parts of himself that he is not comfortable with. This means that he must live his life with the burden of carrying around emotional baggage. This can be very stressful.

For those of you who are introspective, and for those of you who have not been but would like to be, here is an exercise you can use to learn more about yourself. The exercise is simple. All you have to do is get a blank piece of paper and write down your answers to the questions below. This list contains questions that will stimulate thinking about your thoughts, feelings, and beliefs. Whenever possible, try to relate your answers to the stressful objects, events, or situations in your life.

- How would I describe myself as a person?
- What are my strong points?
- What are my weak points?

- Do I see myself as a supportive person? Why?
- Am I receptive to support from others? Why?
- What is the biggest source of stress in my life?
- What do I do that creates the most stress for me?
- What do others do that creates stress for me?
- How do I typically handle stress?
- What were the most effective stress-management strategies I have used in the past?
- Who are the people in my personal and occupational life with whom I am not communicating well?
- If they were to hear what I had to tell them, what would I want them to hear?
- What are my views regarding myself and others flying when not feeling up to par?
- If my life were to be relatively stress-free, what would it look like?
- What secrets have I been carrying around about myself that I haven't told anybody?
- What would happen if I told somebody something about myself that I have never told anybody?
- What one thing is different about me from my friends?
- Who is the most important person in my life?
- What is the most important object in my life?
- If my life were different, how would it be different?
- Whom do I consider to be my best friend? Why?
- Who was the single most influential person in my life?
- What part of my personality would I like to develop?
- What would I like to be like five years from now?
- If I could make the greatest impact on another person's life, who would that person be, and what would I want to do to make such an impact?

You will find that some of these questions got into deep issues for you. They were designed to help you discover parts of yourself you might not have been in touch with. I have found that by discussing these answers with friends, colleagues, and loved ones, pilots are able to increase rapport and intimacy with others. If you should choose to do this, you may find yourself relating more positively to others.

You may at first be uncomfortable opening up to others. If this is the case, go slowly. Keep in mind that the purpose of being open with others is not to tell the entire world everything about yourself. Openness means being genuine with the thoughts, feelings, and beliefs you are willing to share.

Facing Your Issues

An issue is an underlying and unresolved part of a person's personality, beliefs, experiences, or behavior that can be the source of problems in his life. They are also the source of much of the stress that pilots experience.

We all have issues in our lives that must be faced to manage stress effectively. Some of the issues pilots have been willing to share with me include:

- Habits such as smoking, drinking, or drug use
- Inability to get along with others
- Repressed anger and hostility
- Sexuality
- Negativity
- Vulnerability to rejection
- Conflict with parents
- Marital problems
- Procrastination
- Incest victimization and other forms of abuse
- Inability to have or maintain close relationships
- Fears
- Past trauma
- Self-esteem
- Depression
- Jealousy
- Occupational burnout

This list does not fit any of the glamorous stereotypes of the past and present-day aviator. Instead, these are only some of the real issues faced by real people.

As in dealing with any problem, we must identify the issues that may be creating stress in our lives and own up to them. Talking to others about them and taking steps to resolve them would be the next important steps. There are many self-help books available that can help guide you toward resolution. You may also use the problem-solving approach outlined in Chapter 11 to help you develop your own action plan.

INTERACTING WITH OTHERS

Many of the stressors in a pilot's life come about through his interaction with others. Communication is the basis of all of the pilot's interactions.

When channels of communication are open, the pilot is both heard by others and hears what others have to say. This provides a free exchange of information that can be used for decision making, problem solving, and other activities.

When the communication process is blocked, communication channels become closed. This puts stress on the pilot, who can no longer be heard or hear what others have to say. For interaction with others to be less stressful, communication channels must remain open. There are several things that can be done to accomplish this.

Listening to Others

Self-expression is a natural, healthy state that can reflect high self-esteem and a sense of belonging in the world.

What is often missed in self-expression is that it is an important part of communication, which is a process that involves two-way interaction. Expressing without allowing others to express translates into "talking at" others rather than "interacting with" them. People who are poor listeners generally shut down the ability to listen in others. Why? Because other people have a need to express themselves too.

The pilot who is a poor listener tends to increase his own stress with this habit. He doesn't hear what others have to say, and winds up missing out on input and feedback from others that could make life a lot simpler. This pilot will tend to focus on his own ideas, perceptions, and observations, and be blind to information from others. We all have blind spots in our lives that we are not aware of, and we can become aware of them only when others see them and share their observations with us.

Another problem can exist when the pilot is the type of person who remains silent and does not express himself. This type of pilot will keep everybody around him wondering what he is thinking. If he is the pilot in command, and his crew is forced to second-guess him, confusion will prevail in the cockpit. This means more stress for everybody.

Listening is an active process. It not only involves hearing what is being said, but also considering what is being communicated by others. It helps the pilot make more effective decisions because he is able to have more information on which to base his decisions; and it encourages others to listen to him because he is more attentive to what they have to say. Some guidelines for effective listening are provided in Table 12-1.

Table 12–1
Guidelines for Effective Listening

---

1. Make eye contact with the person who is speaking if the situation permits it.
2. Don't interrupt the person to whom you are listening.
3. Don't allow yourself to become distracted.
4. Acknowledge understanding of what is being communicated to you, either verbally or by nodding your head.
5. Ask for more information if you want to hear more about a topic in the conversation.
6. Clarify points that you are not sure you understand.

Communicating More Directly

When we communicate our observations, ideas, and opinions clearly and directly, others will have an opportunity to know where we are coming from right away. This doesn't necessarily mean that they will understand or agree with what we have to say. What it does mean is that the communication will be more direct and less indecisive.

Direct communication translates into more rapid communication. When communication is indirect and wordy, others tune out. If you are a pilot with a tendency to be overly wordy when you communicate with others, half of what you say is probably not being heard. Practice saying what you have to say in fewer words.

Disagreement

All communication is open to disagreement. No two people will agree on everything. When disagreements arise, willingness to place yourself in the other person's position can help you gain a perspective that you may not have considered. I have found that many pilots try so hard to avoid being "wrong" that they ignore the reality of the situation with which they are faced. This can be dangerous and usually creates stress. The pilot who manages his stress effectively is willing to look at both sides of a disagreement and make compromises where they are appropriate. This creates a win-win situation for everyone involved and can drastically reduce stress.

Support

Providing support to others and being receptive to it can be a tremendous stress-management tool. Support is a nonjudgmental way of communicating to others that you are concerned with the experience they are going through and you are behind them all the way. Very few people are able to accomplish important things in their lives without emotional support from others. Once you have been supported by another person or other people, it is important to thank them for the support they gave you.

Briefings

Crew briefings can help increase communication, efficiency, and safety in flight. They can also help reduce stress. Every flight should routinely include two briefings and a debriefing—preflight and en route briefings, and a postflight debriefing. Each briefing should address the operational aspects of the flight and the human factors aspects of the flight. Information that should be included in each briefing is outlined in Table 12-2.

Table 12–2
Flight Crew Briefings

I. Preflight Briefing

   A. *Operational Information That May Affect the Flight*

      Weather—departure, en route, destination
      NOTAMS
      Inoperative aircraft equipment
      Route selected
      Navaids inoperative en route
      Fuel requirements
      Anticipated delays
      Unusual conditions that may affect flight
      Other information deemed relevant by the owner,
         operator, or crew

   B. *Human Factors Information That May Affect the Flight*

      Crewmember mental and physical status
      Crew expectations regarding roles and duties
      Concerns, worries, or issues the crewmember may be
         bringing into the work environment (for example,
         an argument he has just had with his spouse)

II. En Route Briefing

   A. *Operational Information That May Affect the Flight*

      Information reflecting the status of the flight (for
         example, information about navigation, weather,
         altitude, etc.)
      Information about problems that have developed en
         route
      Update information reflecting changes that have
         occurred
      Planning information (such as review of approach charts,
         ATIS information, etc.)

   B. *Human Factors Information That May Affect the Flight*

      Crewmember observations
      Crewmember concerns

Table 12-2 *(Continued)*

III. Postflight Debriefing

The postflight debriefing should address the events that occurred during the flight that were routine, and those that weren't routine. Crewmember expectations that were addressed at the preflight briefing should be examined and evaluated. Where problems existed in crew coordination, the briefing should focus on ways to remedy these problems. Each crewmember's performance should be evaluated in a supportive manner. In addition, each crewmember should be given the opportunity to provide his own input at the debriefing. In summary, the debriefing session should address what worked, what didn't work, and what can be done to make the flight go more smoothly next time.

13

Exercise and Nutrition

There is a saying in aviation that the captain's seat is larger than the first officer's. Fortunately, this saying does not always hold true. But it does raise the question of fitness and nutrition. Because fitness and nutrition are intimately connected with our physical and emotional well-being, we must consider these topics a vital part of stress management for the pilot.

EXERCISE

The Benefits of Exercise

Exercise has many benefits for the pilot. These include greater stamina and endurance, healthier cardiovascular and respiratory systems, and improved general health. Exercise can also serve to help the pilot overcome a sedentary life-style (which is very easy to fall into) and increase reserve strength that can be helpful in assisting him to deal with high-intensity stressors without placing undue energy on the heart. Proper exercise can help create healthy physical conditioning of the body, which will contribute to healthy mental conditioning.

Type of Exercise

Three types of exercises should be included in the pilot's fitness regimen: aerobics, calisthenics, and strength-building exercises.

Aerobic exercise increases oxygen intake into the body, increases blood circulation, and causes the heart to work harder, thus expanding the blood vessels. Examples of aerobic exercises include swimming, walking, jogging, cycling, rope skipping, dancing, and karate.

Calisthenics, or stretching exercises, both improve the flexibility and the range of flexibility of muscles, tendons, and joints. Other forms of exercise should be preceded by calisthenics, for calisthenics prepare the body for vigorous physical activity.

Strength-building exercise helps build the body's muscular strength. Two types of strength-building exercise exist: isotonics and isometrics. In isometric exercise, the muscles are contracted against a stationary object. This object can be a wall, post, or anything else that will not move. This form of exercise increases strength, but does not increase muscle size. Isotonic exercise involves contraction of the muscles against a nonstationary object. Lifting weights, sit-ups, pull-ups, and push-ups all fall into this category of strength-building exercise. These exercises do tend to increase muscle size.

How Often Should I Exercise?

Too little exercise can lead to cardiovascular disease, respiratory problems, muscular degeneration, decreased joint and tendon flexibility, and, of course, stress. Too much exercise can also cause problems. The key to reaping the positive benefits of an exercise program is regularity. If you exercise on a regular basis you will be able to increase your stamina, strength, and flexibility. For most people, it is suggested that they engage in physical exercise three to five times per week.

When Should I Exercise?

It has been found that the time of day does not matter. It is helpful to exercise at the same time every day, but this is often not practical for the pilot. Some pilots have told me that they make it a habit to exercise at the beginning or the middle of the day because if they exercise in the evening, they find it difficult to fall asleep. You will have to determine what works best for you.

Some Precautions Regarding Exercise

For exercise to be safe and beneficial, several precautions must be observed:

1. **Physical Examination**—Before any exercise routine is initiated, a physical examination by a medical doctor is a must. Your doctor can determine what forms of exercise are safest for you to engage in, and how often they can safely be done. Working with your doctor can help you avoid problems.

2. **Don't Overdo It**—When you first start your exercise routine, don't try to move too fast. Go slowly. It is important to work your way up to longer distances, more weight, more repetitions, etc. If you become exhausted, weak, nauseated, or experience pain, you are overdoing it. When these symptoms are experienced, discontinue exercising and go slower next time.

3. **Warm Up Before and Cool Down After Exercising**—Warming up helps your body prepare itself for strenuous exercise. Many injuries and serious problems

can be avoided with a proper warm-up. A five-minute warm-up period before exercise can do wonders for the body. Just as important as the warm-up is the cool-down period. After exercise, the body has to make a gradual adjustment to rest. The body has to wind down slowly. If this winddown period does not take place, serious problems may occur. A five-minute period of slower exercise can help the body cool down.

4. **Don't Exercise When Ill or Injured**—Exercising when you are ill or injured will only put you in the position of possibly worsening your condition. It is better to wait until your body has returned to a healthy state before engaging in strenuous exercise. Once you are healthy, remember to take the time to work up slowly to the point that you were at before the onset of your illness or injury.

NUTRITION

Many of the pilots with whom I have spoken who showed indications of pilot stress were unaware of the daily nutritional requirements that help people maintain their health. When placed on a healthy nutritional regimen, many of them experienced a reduction in their stress symptoms. From these observations, we can say that proper nutrition can play a vital role in the prevention, reduction, and management of pilot stress.

Irregular eating habits, unpredictable schedules, and jet lag are factors that contribute to the pilot's poor nutritional habits. But if stress is to be managed effectively, the body must have its nutritional needs met. These needs require daily intake of the proper amount of carbohydrates, fats, proteins, fiber, water, vitamins, and minerals.

Carbohydrates

Carbohydrates are the main source of the body's energy. They also provide necessary energy for normal brain and central nervous system functioning.

There are two types of carbohydrates: simple and complex. Simple carbohydrates are found in refined sugar and white flour, and contain empty calories. Complex carbohydrates have greater nutritional value and are found in sources such as beans, wheat, fruits, carrots, potatoes, and corn.

Fats

Fats are essential to the development of the pilot's immune system. They are also a form of energy reserve, are important for cellular structures, and insulate the body from heat loss. Fats should not be consumed in excess, as they cause high blood-cholesterol levels. Sources of fat include butter, margarine, salad dressings, dairy products, nuts, meats, chocolate, and fried foods.

Proteins

Proteins are necessary for building and maintaining body tissues, hormone development, digestion, and development of antibodies to fight disease. Sources of protein include animal and fish flesh, cow's milk, and cheese, eggs, and meat. The pilot should be aware that too much protein in the diet tends to be converted to sugar and fat.

Fiber

Fiber constitutes the roughage that is necessary for a healthy diet. An indigestible component of the diet, fiber serves to cleanse the digestive tract, prevent ulcers, constipation, and coronary heart disease. The main sources of fiber are fruits and vegetables, whole grains, and cereals.

Water

At least eight glasses of water per day should be consumed. This will provide the pilot with diluting of blood thickening (which occurs during stress), hydration, assistance with digestion, and elimination of waste materials. Water consumption will also help to minimize the effects of high-altitude flight and jet lag.

Vitamins

Certain vitamins tend to be depleted from the body during stressful periods. These include vitamins C, E, and the B-complex group (see Table 13-1).

Vitamin C (ascorbic acid). Vitamin C, a water-soluble vitamin, is used by the body to repair tissue cells and blood vessels, heal wounds, decrease cholesterol, and lower the incidence of blood clotting. The adult RDA (Recommended Daily Allowance) is 60 mg per day. Sources include freshly squeezed orange juice, citrus fruits, cauliflower, cabbage, sweet potatoes, and tomatoes.

Vitamin E (tocopherol). Vitamin E, a fat-soluble vitamin, provides oxygenation to the cells, aids in reducing blood pressure, reduces fatigue, and prevents and dissolves blood clotting. The adult RDA is 8 to 10 IUs (International Units) for men and 12 IUs for women. Sources include vegetable oils, pears, apples, eggs, almonds, and walnuts.

Table 13-1
The B-Complex Vitamins

Vitamin	RDA (Adult)
B1 (Thiamin)	1.5 mg
B2 (Riboflavin)	1.7 mg (men)/1.2–1.3 mg (women)
Niacin	16.9 mg (men)/13–14 mg (women)
B6 (Pyridoxine)	2.2 mg (men)/2 mg (women)
B12 (Cobalamin)	3.0 micrograms
Biotin	100–200 micrograms

Source: Winter, A., and Winter, R. (1988) *Eat Right, Be Bright.* New York: St. Martin's Press.

The B-Complex Vitamins. The B-complex vitamins serve various body functions including maintenance of nerve functioning, synthesis of DNA, neurochemical transmission, red-blood-cell production, and energy regulation. Sources of B-complex vitamins include fruits, seafoods, milk, eggs, liver, kidneys, butter, cheese, and vegetables. For RDA information, see Table 13-1.

Minerals

Three important minerals tend to be depleted from the body during stress. These are magnesium, iron, and zinc.

Magnesium. Magnesium serves the functions of converting blood sugar (glucose) into energy, maintaining a healthy cardiovascular system, helping the body fight depression, and maintaining muscle, nerve, liver, and kidney functioning. Sources include oatmeal, tofu, spinach, beef, brown rice, lemons, apples, dark-green vegetables, and nuts. The RDA is 350 to 400 mg for men and 300 mg for women.

Iron. Iron helps produce hemoglobin, increases resistance to disease, and wards off fatigue. Sources of iron include clams, eggs, prune juice, tomato juice, beans, meat, and fowl. The RDA is 18 mg per day for adults.

Zinc. Zinc is essential for enzyme and cellular maintenance, aids in healing injuries to the body, and plays a major role in protein synthesis. Sources of zinc include beef, lamb, eggs, oatmeal, brown rice, and seafood. The RDA is 15 mg per day for adults.

14

Conclusion

In this book I have presented an in-depth examination of the causes and effects of Pilot Stress Syndrome. I have also presented a comprehensive approach for managing this stress syndrome.

This book has examined the pilot within the context of the family, the small group (inside the cockpit), and the organizational, social, and sociocultural environments.

There are two reasons for making such an examination. First, the pilot does not function on the job independently from others. Thus a systems perspective was in order, calling for the acknowledgment that every element of a system affects every other element of that system. Here it is clear that the pilot is only one element of the various systems of which he is a part (for example, the pilot's family, organization, social group, etc.).

Secondly, the pilot does not operate in independent systems. Every system of which he is a part will influence and be influenced by every other system to which he belongs. With this in mind, it is not surprising that the pilot's domestic problems can influence decisions and actions taken in the cockpit environment.

"Pilot Stress Syndrome" is the label provided for the complex interplay of factors that can cause mental and physical degeneration in the cockpit. Others have not addressed the nature of stress among pilots in terms of its synergistic effects. This is, however, important since the errors pilots make in the cockpit can lead to a geometric, rather than a linear, progression of events that may endanger the safety of the flight.

The potential benefits for stress management among pilots thus seem clear and are summarized below.

BENEFITS FOR THE PILOT

Management of pilot stress may have many benefits for the pilot. These include decreased stress and anxiety, better interpersonal relations, improved communication skills, better health, greater job satisfaction, increased motivation, freedom from occupational burnout, effective problem-solving tools, a more fulfilling marriage (or relationship with a significant other), greater job stability, increased self-esteem and confidence, and a more positive attitude toward life in general.

BENEFITS FOR THE ORGANIZATION

With a team of pilots possessing the above qualities, the organization should benefit. Greater mental and physical health are reflected in lower insurance and medical costs, decreased absenteeism, and increased safety. The frequency of aircraft accident and incident occurrences should decrease.

The organization would also benefit from better employer/employee relations, better relations among employees, improved service, improved flight-crew efficiency, and a sense of esprit de corps within the organization. This, in turn, can translate into financial gain for the organization.

BENEFITS FOR THE MILITARY

Many of the benefits found in the organization apply to the military services as well. Other benefits can also be derived from stress management for military pilots. These include smoother mission coordination and implementation, fewer aircraft and flight-crew losses during training and actual missions, more efficient and responsive line of defense, a decreased washout and dropout rate in flight-training centers, improved leadership, lower incidence of drug and alcohol use and abuse, and increased tolerance to combat missions.

BENEFITS OF THIS PROGRAM

The approach to management of pilot stress presented in this book has a number of benefits that are lacking in traditional stress-management approaches. First and foremost, it recognizes the importance of the pilot's role as a viable and necessary human resource in aviation. The pilot's knowledge, skills, and abilities must be supported and cultivated in order to assist him to grow in his profession. With this increased development, professional aviation grows and improves.

Second, it recognizes the pilot's personal needs. The private life of the pilot can be highly stressful. By providing tools that can be effectively applied in the pilot's personal daily life, this stress-management approach can help the pilot as an individual.

The third benefit of the program involves acknowledg-

ing the pilot as a professional. Through extensive research in the field of aviation, this approach to pilot
stress management is geared specifically to the pilot. This
is accomplished through a deep and intense understanding of the issues that face pilots. It is also accomplished
through use of language that pilots understand and use
in their daily lives.

The fourth benefit to be derived from this approach is
its flexibility. It can meet the demands of any segment of
aviation.

THE THIRD REVOLUTION IN AVIATION

It is my hope that this book has provided you with insight into the problems pilots face that lead to stress. As
an active observer and participant in aviation, I have
had an opportunity to experience firsthand what I feel
is the third revolution in aviation safety. The first revolution involved the acknowledgment of human factors
as a critical element in aviation safety. This opened the
door to a serious look at the way in which man and
machine interface. It also opened the door to evolution
of the second revolution, which was marked by the introduction of Cockpit Resource Management (CRM),
which not only acknowledged the importance of man/
machine interaction, but also the interaction among humans. The CRM approach is an interactional (or interpersonal) one. I am now suggesting that the field of
aviation safety is experiencing its third revolution. This
is marked by the tendency toward greater self-examina-
tion by the pilot.

This third revolution, which is marked by introspection in aviation, is an important step in aviation safety.
The pilot is more willing now than he ever has been to

take a close look at himself and acknowledge that he is a psychological being who can take responsibility in his role in aviation safety. It is my hope that *Managing Pilot Stress* will make a big difference in this exciting revolution.

REFERENCES

Chapter 1
Selye, H. (1956) *The Stress of Life*. New York: McGraw-Hill.

Chapter 3
Aerospace Safety. (1979) "Who's Flying the Airplane?" *Aerospace Safety, 8,* 14–15.

Baddeley, A. (1972) "Selective Attention and Performance in Dangerous Environments." *British Journal of Psychology, 63,* 537–546.

Friedman, M., and Rosenman, R. (1959) "Association of Specified Overt Behavior Pattern With Blood and Cardiovascular Findings." *Journal of the American Medical Association, 169,* 1286–1296.

Hart, S., and Hauser, J. (1987) "Inflight Application of Three Pilot Workload Measurement Techniques." *Aviation, Space and Environmental Medicine, 58*(5), 402–410.

Mandler, G. (1967) "Invited Commentary." In M. H. Appley & R. Trumbull, Eds., *Psychological Stress: Issues in Research.* New York: Appleton Century Crofts.

Richardson, J. (1978) "Takeoffs and Judgment." *Aerospace Safety, 3,* 20–21.

Ruffell-Smith, H. (1967) "Heart Rate of Pilots Flying Aircraft on Scheduled Airline Routes." *Aerospace Medicine, 38,* 1117–1119.

Santilli, S. (1979) "Doing What Comes Naturally." *Aerospace Safety*, *8*, 10–11.

U.S. Department of Transportation—Federal Aviation Administration. *Aviation Instructor's Handbook*. Advisory Circular 61–14. Wyoming: Aviation Maintenance Publishers.

Walker, F. (1979) "Pilot Error: The Why Behind the Words." *Aerospace Safety*, *3*, 4–5.

Wertheimer, M. (1979) "Principles of Organization." In R. Lundin, Ed. *Theories and Systems of Psychology* (2nd ed.) (pp. 226–227). Lexington, MA: D. C. Heath and Company. (Original work published 1923.)

Chapter 4

Fine, P., and Hartman, B. (1968) "Psychiatric Strengths and Weaknesses of Typical Air Force Pilots." *Technical Report 68–121*. Brooks AFB, TX: USAF School of Aerospace Medicine.

Friedman, M., and Rosenman, R. (1959) "Association of Specified Overt Behavior Pattern With Blood and Cardiovascular Findings." *Journal of the American Medical Association, 169*, 1286–1296.

Johnston, N. (1985) "Occupational Stress and the Professional Pilot: The Role of the Pilot Advisory Group (PAG)." *Aviation, Space and Environmental Medicine, 56*(7), 633–637.

Reinhardt, R. (1967) "The Flyer Who Fails: An Adult Situational Reaction." *American Journal of Psychiatry, 124*, 48–52.

Chapter 5

Booze, C., and Staggs, C. (1987) "A Comparison of Postmortem Coronary Atherosclerosis Findings in General Aviation Pilot Fatalities." *Aviation, Space and Environmental Medicine, 58*(4), 297–300.

Department of Transportation. (1974) *Medical Handbook for Pilots*. Washington, D.C.: U.S. Government Printing Office. 05-007-0025408.

Diagram Visual Information, Ltd. (1977) *Man's Body: An Owner's Manual*. New York: Bantam Books.

Guyton, A. (1979) *Physiology of the Human Body* (5th ed.) Philadelphia: W. B. Saunders Company.

Ehret, C., and Scanlon, L. (1986) *Overcoming Jet Lag*. New York: Berkley Books.

Girdano, A., and Everly, G. (1979) *Controlling Stress and Tension: A Holistic Approach.* Englewood Cliffs, NJ: Prentice Hall, Inc.

Hanson, P. (1986) *The Joy of Stress.* Kansas City, MO: Andrews, McMeel & Parker.

Holt, G., Taylor, W., and Carter, E. (1985) "Airline Pilot Disability: The Continued Experience of a Major U.S. Airline." *Aviation, Space and Environmental Medicine, 56*(10), 939–944.

Kinney, J., and Leaton, G. (1983) *Loosening the Grip: A Handbook of Alcohol Information.* St. Louis: The C. V. Mosby Company.

Mindell, E. (1979) *Vitamin Bible.* New York: Warner Books.

Strughold, H. (1971) *Your Body Clock.* New York: Charles Scribner's Sons.

Weinstein, M. C., and Stason, W. B., Eds. (1976) *Hypertension: A Policy Perspective.* Cambridge: Harvard University Press.

Chapter 6

Black, A. (1983) "Psychiatric Illness in Military Pilots." *Aviation, Space and Environmental Medicine, 54*(7), 595–598.

Cooper, C., and Sloan, S. (1985) "The Sources of Stress on the Wives of Commercial Airline Pilots." *Aviation, Space and Environmental Medicine, 56*(4), 317–321.

DeVany, A., and Garges, E. (1972) "A Forecast of Air Travel and Airport Use in 1980." *Transportation Research, 1.*

Foushee, H. (1982) "The Role of Communications, Sociopsychological, and Personality Factors in the Maintenance of Crew Coordination." *Aviation, Space and Environmental Medicine, 53*(11), 1062–1066.

Hodge, P. (1985) "Thermal Stress." *Flying Safety, 8,* 8–11.

Jacks, R. (1978) "Crew Coordination." *Aerospace Safety, 12,* 4–6.

Moore, T. (1986) "U.S. Airline Deregulation: Its Effects on Passengers, Capital, and Labor." *The Journal of Law and Economics, 29*(19), 1–28.

Rogers, A. (1986) "U.S. Airlines Are Flying High on Merger Mania." *Purchasing, 101*(2), 56–60.

Shultz, D. (1982) *Psychology and Industry Today: An Introduction to Industrial and Organizational Psychology* (3rd ed.). New York: Macmillan.

Welles, C., Payne, S., Seghers, F., and Ichniowski, T. (1986) "Is Deregulation Working?" *Business Week,* (December 22), 50–55.

Chapter 7

American Psychiatric Association. (1987) *Diagnostic and Statistical Manual of Mental Disorders* (3rd ed., revised) Washington, D.C.: APA.

Duvall, E. (1977) "The Traditional Family Life Cycle." In I. Goldenberg and H. Goldenberg (1985) *Family Therapy: An Overview* (2nd ed.) (p. 19). Monterey, CA: Brooks/Cole Publishing Company.

Kübler-Ross, E. (1969) *On Death and Dying.* New York: Macmillan.

Maslow, A. (1943) "A Theory of Human Motivation." *Psychological Review, 50,* 370–396.

Sloan, S., and Cooper, C. (1986) "Stress Coping Strategies in Commercial Airline Pilots." *Journal of Occupational Medicine, 28*(1), 49–52.

Chapter 10

Davis, M., Eshelman, E., and McKay, M. (1982) *The Relaxation and Stress Reduction Workbook.* Oakland, CA: New Harbinger Publications.

Jacobson, E. (1974) *Progressive Relaxation.* Chicago: The University of Chicago Press, Midway Reprint.

Chapter 11

Hunsaker, P., and Alessandra, A. (1980) *The Art of Managing People.* Englewood Cliffs, NJ: Prentice-Hall, Inc.

Kreitner, R. (1986) *Management* (3rd ed.). Dallas: Houghton Mifflin.

Chapter 13

Cooper, K. (1970) *The New Aerobics.* New York: Bantam Books.

Executive Health Examiners, Eds. (1985) *Stress Management for the Executive.* New York: Berkley Books.

Hanson, P. (1986) *The Joy of Stress.* Kansas City, MO: Andrews, McMeel & Parker.

Mindell, E. (1979) *Vitamin Bible.* New York: Warner Books.

Swarth, J. (1986) *Stress and Nutrition.* San Diego, CA: Health Media of America, Inc.

Winter, A., and Winter, R. (1988) *Eat Right, Be Bright.* New York: St. Martin's Press.

INDEX